Coping with Relationship Breakdown
A Practical Guide

rrelly BA, MSC Psych, MBA, RCSI, Dip King's Inns is a
t psychotherapist with over twenty years' experience
couples with their relationships. One of Ireland's leading
in the area of marriage and family, he is a graduate of
ity College Dublin, the Royal College of Surgeons and
norable Society of King's Inns. He has lectured in De Paul
ity, All Hallows College and Dublin City University, and
regular media commentator and speaker at international
rences on marriage and family. Previously he was director
nselling with ACCORD, Ireland's largest relationship
nselling agency, and is now clinical director of Achieve Balance
nselling Service (www.achievebalance.ie). He is the author of
od Marriage Guide: The Practical Way to Improve Your
ship (2007) and The Art of Balance: Creating Calm in a
World (2008), both published by Veritas.

Coping with
RELATIONSHIP
BREAKDOWN

A Practical Guide

JOHN FARRELLY

VERITAS

Published 2014 by
Veritas Publications
7–8 Lower Abbey Street
Dublin 1, Ireland
publications@veritas.ie
www.veritas.ie

ISBN 978 1 84730 561 9
Copyright © John Farrelly, 2014

10 9 8 7 6 5 4 3 2 1

A catalogue record for this book is available from the British
Library.

Cover designed by Dara O'Connor, Veritas
Printed in the Republic of Ireland by Hudson Killeen Ltd, Dublin

Veritas books are printed on paper made from the wood pulp
of managed forests. For every tree felled, at least one tree is
planted, thereby renewing natural resources.

Dedicated to my parents Jack and Phyllis,
my wife Laura and our sons Aaron and Ben.

Grant me the serenity to accept the
things I cannot change,
the courage to change the things I can,
and wisdom to know the difference.

Contents

Introduction

Marriage is a bedrock of our civilisation, and in its purest form offers love, health and security to each member of this core unit of society. However, when love breaks down, it is important that we support separating families in coping, recovering and recommencing a happy, balanced life. In a compassionate society every person is entitled to dignity, respect and the possibility of achieving contentment and love. Relationship breakdown is a common and accepted part of modern life, and yet it is an extremely difficult experience, especially when there are children involved.

Bad experiences have the potential to make a person doubt themselves and cast themselves in the role of 'failure'. Yet, overcoming relationship breakdown with the proper support system can reawaken aspects of a person's life that have vanished during a failing marriage or relationship.

I have worked with clients and families for over twenty years as director of the largest marriage and relationship counselling service in Ireland. While researching my first book, *The Good Marriage Way: The Practical Way to Improve Your Relationship* (2008), I spoke to over three thousand married couples. Their optimism that they would live out their days together was awe-inspiring; none of them married with the intention of separating or divorcing.

The cultural script says that we will meet our true love and live happily ever after. However, in reality, maintaining a lifelong intimate relationship is a challenge that can end in disappointment, despite our best intentions. As such, couples are often underprepared and overwhelmed in the face of relationship breakdown.

This book is a practical guide to aid those going through this painful and stressful process. It aims to cut through the fog of confusion, offering pragmatic, clear and achievable guidance to couples, individuals and indeed any person caught up in the turmoil of relationship breakdown. It includes a number of case studies based on my close work with couples over the years, and the learning is underpinned with up-to-date psychological and social research. This book also provides key insights to the legal, health and social care support available to individuals during this challenging time (although it is not intended to replace professional and legal advice). Each chapter provides clear information, advice and coping mechanisms to facilitate the best possible outcome for couples and families affected by the separation or divorce process. The aim is to help the reader to replace the sorrow that a failed relationship brings with confidence and hope for the future.

Chapter One demonstrates why it is imperative to avoid conflict. It looks at how to stop fighting and start thinking in the midst of a relationship breakdown. During this time the ego and emotions can reign supreme; grown adults attack each other until both they and their children are so emotionally (and financially) traumatised that they are forced to stop. Yet the reality is that if adults learn to put aside negative emotion and concentrate on a successful separation, the prospect for both themselves and their family is much brighter. Even when children are grown with families of their own, they still want special family occasions to be spent together without incident. In place of anger and bitterness, this chapter teaches skills and strategies for solving differences.

Chapter Two addresses the recognition and overcoming of grief encountered during relationship breakdown. Grief occurs following all significant loss, not only death. In fact, relationship breakdown is not far behind the death of a loved one in terms of the heartache it causes. Unresolved grief is a key contributor to messy separations and divorces. Caught up in the battlefield of relationship breakdown, couples can fail to realise the many losses they face. Individuals are often forced to give up their home, lose access to their children, lose friends and feel abandoned by family members. They may have to give up cherished activities and let go of some of their life goals. The future they had envisioned for themselves can begin to look very different – separating couples can experience the loss of the people they used to be and the people they thought they would become. This loss is further complicated because it is not usually openly acknowledged, socially accepted or publicly grieved. This chapter helps individuals to recognise and resolve their grief through acceptance and adjustment to their new environment, and suggests ways of reinvesting emotional energy in purposeful activity.

Perhaps the biggest issue raised by separating couples is their negative experience of the courts and legal system. Chapter Three examines alternative approaches to dispute resolution. These approaches have developed as individuals and society learn that the formal adversarial court setting is rarely conducive to solving the problems created by relationship breakdown. Dealing with family matters solely within the legal system can take an extremely long time, during which physical, emotional and financial health are sacrificed. The combative and costly approach underpinning the legal system can leave the ordinary family very bruised and ill-prepared for the future. Rather, evidence suggests that the optimal approach is to aid both individuals to collaborate, listen and agree a mutually beneficial solution before entering the legal system. It is important during this time of huge change to make fair, balanced and rational decisions that meet the needs of all parties. Alternatives, such as counselling, mediation, collaborative law and trial separation, provide routes to resolution other than court proceedings. These collaborative practices can help couples to accept the reality of their relationship and make informed choices as to the best future options for all involved.

Chapter Four examines the challenges and benefits of maintaining links with grandparents and particularly the issues grandparents face in supporting their adult children and grandchildren. As one would expect, most of the literature on the impact of relationship breakdown focuses on the couple in question and their children, yet grandparents seldom escape the distress caused by separation and are often forgotten. Grandparents can provide much-needed emotional and practical support for both adults and children during this time of change. Maintaining the connection between grandparents and grandchildren can be a real challenge; however, grandparents can help to maintain a sense of stability for children, listen to them and offer respite from the turmoil of their own home.

Chapter Five provides and examines techniques to ensure a collaborative approach to parenting. Over 70 per cent of couples seeking relationship counselling have children under the age of eleven; and close to 50 per cent of children in the western world will experience their parents' divorce. Parenting in a loving relationship is not easy, and parenting after separation demands even more commitment and focus. The challenge is to make the ongoing parenting relationship as manageable and as constructive as possible and to pave the way for a smooth transition for both parents and children. Putting aside personal issues to parent amicably can be fraught with stress but the benefits of this approach hugely outweigh the discipline required to work together, ensuring that separated parents can give their children continued stability and closeness during a time of major change. With the right tools, support and frame of mind, it is possible to initiate and maintain a working relationship between separated parents for the sake of the children.

Chapter Six further enhances the collaborative parenting approach and considers the most common problems experienced by children of separating parents. No matter how much a husband and wife grow to dislike each other, most parents' unconditional love for their children moves them to ask themselves some tough questions about what effect their actions might have. They wonder about how the children will make sense of what is happening; how they will react as the family changes. Will they adjust well? Will their performance in school suffer? Will they withdraw from their friends, and perhaps suffer some permanent emotional harm? Does it make a difference what age children are when their parents separate? Or what gender they are? This chapter suggests evidenced-based approaches to addressing problems that arise for children during separation and how to provide a safe space for children of all ages.

Chapters Seven and Eight aim to offer help and support to men and women respectively. How we perceive the world and respond to specific situations can be linked to our gender. Over the years I have watched as women and men pass like ships in the night without truly understanding each other's position or approach to relationships. With this in mind, these chapters demonstrate how, by understanding our partner and ourselves, both parties can exit a relationship with their dignity intact while maintaining hope for the future.

During a relationship breakdown it is very important to gain some measure of control and insight into your internal self. This will give you the psychological strength and balance to deal with external events and challenges as they arise. Chapter Nine sets out a mindful approach to relationship breakdown. Such a traumatic event can leave a person overwhelmed, struggling and questioning their capacity for love and contentment. Yet, it is during our lowest times that we have the opportunity to take a different view of our lives. Many people spend years in search of meaning; few realise that the sorrow of relationship breakdown can be a gateway to choosing a more balanced existence. Individuals who use mindful and meditative coping techniques improve their physical and emotional well-being. This chapter sets out a number of practical mechanisms and processes for engaging in mindful acts which can aid coping and recovery after a relationship breakdown.

This book is designed so that you can pick it up at times of pressure and dip back into specific chapters to overcome certain issues. Keep it near to hand to read on good days and bad! The secret to getting the most out of it is to read, reflect and work to change your behaviour and thinking. When pain, anger or hopelessness descends, we *can* and *do* recover. Personal growth is the key to ensuring a successful outcome to relationship breakdown, after which we can set out on a new path to contentment.

Moving Beyond Conflict

The end of most marriages and long-term relationships affects not only the couple who are breaking up, but also their children and extended family. Many of these relationships have broken down over time and there is a lack of affection, closeness, appreciation and love between the couple in question, which can lead to intense fighting. This gradual emotional estrangement results in an increased sense of apathy and indifference. Initially, couples persevere, despite mounting disillusionment, and attempt to solve their problems by asserting positive feelings or attempting to please their partner. As feelings of anger and hurt increase in frequency and intensity, partners begin to genuinely weigh up whether they should stay or leave, and attempts to please each other generally decrease. Even at this point, many couples struggle on; yet anger increases, trust declines and sense of loneliness and helplessness sets in. Over time, thoughts begin to focus on determining exactly how to end the relationship, and this is the stage at which couples usually seek counselling. Eventually, it may be decided that the pain of ending the relationship is more acceptable than the prolonged pain of remaining together, initiating a separation. A key factor and indicator of success is the degree to which separating adults can learn to put aside negative emotion and concentrate on as amicable a separation as possible. Working through conflict can make us stronger, more resilient and more accepting. This chapter will explain the simple steps couples can take to deal with conflict and ensure that communication is healthy and constructive.

Even when both parties know a relationship is over, instead of collaborating and mediating the best approach, their emotions often reign supreme and battle lines are drawn. This can have an extremely detrimental effect on both individuals and any children involved. A number of studies indicate that the children of parents who were co-operative during a split reported better relationships with their parents, grandparents, step-parents, and siblings. Most research,[1] and my own clinical experience, points to the fact that children want and need relationships with both parents. What children seek is not for their parents to be friends, but that they are cordial and refrain from undermining each other. It is imperative that separating parents put the brakes on fighting and instead grease the wheels of understanding how to avoid unnecessary conflict.

No healthy marriage is free of conflict, so it would be absurd to suggest that the ending of a relationship can be entirely conflict free. Every couple is composed of two people with different experiences, interests and emotional predispositions, regardless of their one-time compatibility. Each individual will have a different perspective on the cause of the relationship breakdown and the solution to the current impasse. Those differences will create conflict, whether it is over money, living arrangements, in-laws,

---

1. K. R. Blaisure and M. J. Geasler, 'Results of a Survey of Court-Connected Parent Educated Programs in U.S. Counties', *Family and Conciliation Review* (1996): 23–40.

property or child-rearing. Some combination of these, and a host of other issues, will necessarily be encountered in ending a relationship.

Conflict is a part of life and can be productive, creating deeper understanding and leading to a solution; or it can be destructive, causing further resentment and hostility. The real issue is how the conflict is resolved, not that it occurs in the first place. It is important that we learn from our behaviour, to avoid carrying our blind spots into new relationships or ignoring our own weaknesses while blaming our former partner for everything. The good news is that each individual can unlearn destructive behaviours and replace them with behaviours that ensure they can co-operate in the best interests of all concerned.

Distrust Your Instinct

Conflict involves strong emotions. People sometimes believe that the venting of these emotions is the best way to 'clear the air'. Yet anger, bitterness and abuse are not good for us. Neither are they good for our partner or children. Instead of resolving our conflicts by creating and implementing a well-conceived plan, we often revert to our primitive instincts by becoming demanding and disrespectful of one another. These instincts not only fail to provide long-term solutions, but also work to destroy any feeling of security that you and your children still have. To stop ourselves from acting on this instinct, we have to apply new principles to the situation.

Understanding Your Own and Your Former Partner's Conflict Style

An important principle in ensuring resolution is acknowledging that we each have our own way of dealing with conflict. To solve conflict we have first to look at and understand ourselves. This can be a hard thing to do, as it can be tempting to believe that it is a former partner's obstinate behaviour that has led to relationship breakdown. The first step to negotiating a stable future is for both parties to be open to the possibility that they are in part responsible for the current situation. This is good news, as it means you have within your control part of the solution.

When you recognise your own and your former partner's conflict style, you save yourself a lot of anxiety and pain. People commonly fall into one of three conflict styles:

Validating: those who like to talk things out.

Volatile: those who like to row.

Avoidant: those who avoid arguments and conflict.

About half of all men – both in their own assessment and in the assessment of their former partners – tend to be avoidant. However, while nearly six out of ten women see themselves as validating, only four out of ten men feel that this is true of their former partners. Similarly, while around two in ten women see themselves as volatile, nearly twice as many men experienced them as volatile. Leaving aside the specific issues over which these couples are in conflict, these findings suggest considerable differences in how former partners perceive each other. In other words, in terms of how they resolve relationship conflict, around 40 per cent of men and women see themselves quite differently from the way their former partner sees them. These findings are consistent with numerous studies that have documented a pattern of demand–withdrawal in unhappy relationships: women are perceived as demanding by men who then withdraw or become aggressive, possibly because women's perceived demands are experienced as a threat, and men's withdrawal is experienced as denial. Put simply, there is a thin line between what is real and what is imagined in broken – indeed all – intimate relationships.

Separating couples often continue to engage in a range of negative behaviours, particularly criticism, insult and failure to listen. This adds considerably to their distress and further damages their potential to dissolve the relationship while ensuring their children are psychologically, socially and economically protected. In addition, the tension between self-perception and how each party is perceived by their former partner is itself indicative of the gap in understanding and communication which has arisen within the relationship.

Although both men and women engage equally in these behaviours, it is the perception of the former partner's behaviour rather than perception of one's own behaviour that is most strongly associated with distress. It is my experience that women tend to be more adversely affected by divergent styles of conflict resolution than men. Female clients often tell me that for years they have had a sense of powerlessness in their relationship, feeling that their partner has been the source of all conflict. When a woman decides to end a relationship, it may be the first time in years that she has felt a sense of control. Men who have an avoidant approach to resolving conflict will, given time, acknowledge that this approach is not in their best interests. However, they often continue this behaviour during the separation period rather than engaging fully in order to ensure the best possible outcome for themselves and their children.

That many separating men and women see and experience each other quite differently from the way they see and experience themselves, results in erosion of empathic understanding. Yet empathy is a key component in ensuring a successful separation. In view of this, counselling before, during and post separation is crucial in restoring common ground, so that the former partners can see and be seen in a clearer, more positive light, both cognitively and emotionally.

Separating couples should seek to avoid falling into the following detrimental patterns:

- Not discussing and agreeing with your former partner the method used to resolve your conflicts.
- Being too invested in getting your own way, or making extreme demands, and therefore not being able to be flexible enough to be fair.
- Forgetting that there are usually several ways of doing things and that your own reality is not the only reality. We humans have a consistent tendency to believe that we are both right and reasonable. You will be much more effective if you are willing to see the other person's point of view.
- Focusing too much on what you could lose and not enough on what you and your children could gain.
- Believing your former partner must lose for you to win.

Women are often more comfortable expressing their feelings to friends. Men often are not as comfortable with emotional sharing. As such, men can be confused when women discuss feelings and emotions, but are usually better at dealing with concrete matters without getting emotional. It is really important to appreciate that our former partners are different from us. Despite how well we think we know someone, we often assume a lot about the way they behave. Stop and answer the following, first of yourself, then of your former partner.

- Am I passive or aggressive or passive aggressive?
- Am I emotional or logical?
- Do I prefer to communicate or do I like to be solitary?
- Do I like to win, or am I happy with a compromise?
- Do I express my feelings to gain understanding, or to find a solution?

Take a step back and try to look at the issue from your former partner's point of view:

- Why might they feel this way?
- How are they feeling right now?
- What can I do to make this easier for them and reach an agreed solution?

If your former partner approaches conflict differently to you, it is not necessarily wrong. By appreciating your differences, you will avoid unnecessary conflict as you end the relationship and move on with your lives.

Communication is Always the Key
The first step to effective communication is listening. Letting your former partner know that you have heard

what they have said is vital. Keep in mind that when we are experiencing anger, fear or sadness, we don't always hear what the other person is saying. Have you ever had an argument with someone and then discussed it at a different time only to discover that neither of you can remember what you were fighting about? It is likely, though, that you can remember whether you were sad, angry or hurt.

It is difficult for most of us to separate our thoughts from our emotions, especially when we are upset. Making that separation is very important. Usually both people have valid points and what is required is compromise. Even during the bitterest of break-ups, compromise and collaboration are possible. A general rule that works well is to talk only when you are both ready to listen. At the point a discussion becomes heated, it is time to pause and leave it for another time.

Breaking Old Habits

It can be difficult to put some of these strategies into play because when we are upset or feeling vulnerable we sometimes protect ourselves with the same defence mechanism over and over again until it becomes habit. Habits, especially old ones, are hard to break. People tend to act the same way or say the same things every time they argue. How many times have you heard the line, 'Why do you always …?' There is a huge difference between saying, 'I hate you because of the stupid things you do' and 'I'm really frustrated with some of the things you do. It makes me feel …' This last statement gets the message across and isn't something you have to apologise for later.

- Think about how you will begin to take responsibility for your part in arguments. Ask how could you change your action or reaction to a problem?

- Ask yourself what your part in the conflict is. Are you too passive, dominant, dependent, independent, aggressive? Do you not listen? Can you be empathic to the other person's feelings?
- List your most common negative reactions.
- Decide to change them one at a time.
- Don't expect immediate results. Be consistent and realistic in your actions and reactions.
- Learn to nurture yourself. Do things that make you feel good physically, emotionally and psychologically, because making changes requires a great deal of energy.

Our first impulse is to push the point that we are right and win the argument at any cost. Finding a peaceful resolution can be difficult, if not impossible, when both parties stubbornly stick to their guns. It helps if each person decides to try listening to each other and negotiating instead:

- Work out if the issue is worth fighting over.
- Try to separate the problem from the person.
- Resist the urge to bring up other unresolved but unrelated issues.
- Try to stay calm. Cool off first if you feel too angry to talk calmly.
- Keep in mind that the idea is to resolve the conflict, not to win the argument. Try to put emotions aside.
- Remember that the other party isn't obliged to agree with you on everything.
- Define the problem and stick to the topic.
- Respect the other person's point of view by paying attention and listening.

- Communicate your side of the story clearly and honestly.
- Try to find points of common ground.
- Don't interrupt your former partner while they are speaking. Actively listen to what they are saying and what they mean. Check that you understand them by asking questions.
- Agree to disagree.

Once both parties understand the views of each other, misunderstandings can be avoided. These small wins add up over time and create a good platform for restoring trust and ensuring all in the separated family do not have to endure needless stress and anxiety.

In all conflict, a key approach is to generate several possible solutions. This is a creative integrative process. The emphasis should be on the things you both agree on and on your shared goals. This can open up several possible solutions. It is important to avoid evaluating and judging each idea until it looks as though no other alternatives can be suggested. You can then evaluate the alternatives and eliminate those that are not acceptable to either of you. At this stage in the process you must both be honest and willing to say things like, 'I wouldn't be happy with that' or 'I don't think that would be fair to me.' Keep narrowing them down until you are left with the one that seems best for you both. Make certain there is a mutual commitment to the decision.

Implementing an agreed approach will be hard, and it is one thing to arrive at a decision, another to carry it out. Talk about how it will be put into action. Who is responsible for doing what and by when? Not all agreed-upon solutions turn out to be as good as initially expected. Make it routine to ask your former partner how the solution is working and how they are feeling about it. Something may have been overlooked or misjudged; or something unexpected may have occurred since the decision was made. Both of you should understand that the decision is always open for revision, but that modifications have to be agreed upon.

Ideas for Identifying and Avoiding Conflict Hotspots

Remember your triggers: Make a list of your 'hot buttons' – events or topics that trigger your anger. Review the list periodically to mentally prepare for controlling your temper when these issues arise.

Choose your battles: Ask yourself, 'Is it worth arguing about?' If you feel that working through the disagreement is more important than maintaining the peace, then speak up. But if the debate is going to create more problems than it solves, remain silent or change the subject.

Acknowledge disagreement: Sometimes you can keep a conflict from escalating simply by acknowledging your disagreement. When you say, 'Well, that's frustrating. I was hoping we would agree on the subject', you give everyone a chance to stop and think before continuing to argue.

Have a plan: Make another list, this time of the things you can do to calm down in the wake of conflict: take a walk, clear your desk, listen to music, and so on. Keep the list handy and refer to it after you've walked away from the dispute.

Tips for Keeping Conflict Under Control

Calm down with controlled breathing: Anger and stress cause rapid breathing, which can deplete your oxygen, raise your blood pressure and cloud your judgement. Reduce your stress by slowly breathing in through your nose and out through your mouth.

Stop talking and listen: Practice the 'shut up and listen' technique. While controlling your breathing, be quiet and listen to what the other person has to say.

Find a point of agreement: Find something in the other person's position to agree with, and tell them. They'll know that you are trying to understand their point of view, and they may be more willing to listen to yours.

Don't take it personally: Don't make the conflict about you or the other person, make it about the issue at hand. Use an 'I' statement to objectify the conflict, as in, 'I think we have different ideas about the best way to approach this' or 'I understand that you really think it's better this way.' Then ask for feedback: 'Am I hearing you correctly?'

Focus on one issue at a time: Don't fall into the overload trap. Concentrate on the here and now and don't be tempted to list all your former partner's perceived failings to them. Instead of saying, 'We cannot go to the school play together next week, because you're always late picking up the children, and they get upset', you might say, 'Let's talk about the best way to ensure the children go to and enjoy their school play.'

Avoid judgemental statements: If you blurt out mocking or antagonistic statements, you will only cause the other person to stop listening and become angry. The statement, 'I think it would be better if we do it this way', is less judgmental than 'You're doing it all wrong.'

Forget about winning and losing: Work to find a resolution that allows both sides to emerge from the conflict satisfied.

When you stop trying to 'defeat your opponent' you'll be more receptive to good ideas and resolve conflicts quicker.

Don't try to change what you can't change: You can't force others to agree with you, so don't keep arguing in an attempt to do so. You can't change the past, so don't get caught up in a conflict about something that has already happened.

Be respectful: You insult others when you immediately dismiss their ideas or suggestions. If you have your doubts, ask the person to explain how their proposal will work. If you still disagree, ask, 'Why do you want to do it that way?' When you understand another's motives, it is easier to find a resolution that will be acceptable to you both.

Be willing to be wrong: Do your research, review the facts with an open mind, and then be willing to admit it if you find that you're wrong. That can eliminate lingering hostility and indeed make others feel more comfortable admitting their own mistakes.

Apologise for offences: If you have offended the other person, be sure to apologise. A simple, 'I'm sorry I raised my voice' is enough to express your regret and to set the bar for respectful treatment.

Walk away: If you simply cannot find a way to resolve the conflict, agree to disagree and then walk away. Work through your list of ideas for calming down and, if necessary, talk to a trusted friend or advisor for emotional support.

Don't waste the opportunities for personal and professional growth presented by healthy conflict. After you've resolved a disagreement, take time to acknowledge the good work both of you have done. It is helpful to show your appreciation and express your gratitude for the time and effort your former partner has invested in resolving the dispute. After you've successfully resolved a dispute, take the time to reflect on the disagreement, its causes and its resolution. The more you learn about managing conflicts and disagreements, the better able you will be to negotiate, compromise and emerge from disputes in the future.

Gift Forgiveness

Forgiveness is an essential part of any marriage and relationship. It is an equally essential aspect of any successful separation. Forgiveness is a decision. Once you decide to forgive your former partner, the anger and sadness inside you will begin to dissipate. The regard and trust you once had will not return, but you will begin to have a greater sense of balance and perspective. Forgiveness means never bringing up the issue again. If you are forgiving something, don't dwell on it anymore. Forgiveness takes time. You shouldn't rush into a flippant forgiveness, nor should you withhold it. Forgiveness is a gift, to your former partner, yourself and to your children. Your ex-partner cannot demand or expect it and should be grateful for it.

Overcoming Your Grief

Grief occurs after any type of significant loss, not only following a death. While death is the ultimate loss, the emotional impact caused by the end of a marriage is not far behind for the majority of adults and children involved. The fact of the matter is that unrecognised and unresolved grief can be a key contributor to messy separations and divorces. Caught up in the battlefield of separation, many separating people fail to realise the multiplicity of losses they are facing. During relationship breakdown individuals may be forced to give up their home, lose full-time access to their children, lose friends and even family members. They may have to give up cherished activities and groups and to let go of some of their life hopes and goals, effectively losing the future they had envisioned for themselves.

The loss surrounding relationship breakdown is further complicated because it is what is termed a 'disenfranchised grief'. No matter how progressive modern society claims to be, the grief caused by relationship breakdown is not always acknowledged or socially supported, and separation and divorce are still frowned upon and deemed unacceptable within many families and communities. When a loved one or family member dies, grieving rituals surround and ease the pain of the loss. These rituals also create a space to feel and accept the loss. However, there are no rituals in place to deal with the grief caused by relationship breakdown. A separating family and couple receive no cards, flowers or expressions of sympathy. At the end of a marriage, things that were once valuable are irretrievably lost, and there is nothing to validate that loss.

A definition of loss is 'the fact of no longer having something, or of having less of something that was once cherished'. This definition simply and elegantly identifies the basis for the unique reactions to loss. During separation, a broad range of grief-induced emotions, thoughts and behaviours may occur. These include:

- Feelings of numbness, sadness, anger, guilt, anxiety, despair, loneliness, powerlessness, yearning, freedom and relief.
- Physical sensations of shock, such as fatigue, hollow stomach, aching limbs, dry mouth, breathlessness, tightness in the throat and chest and sensitivity to noise.
- Thoughts of disbelief, confusion and disorientation.
- Behaviours such as sleep disturbance and lack of appetite.
- Absentmindedness, crying, sighing, restless overactivity, searching.

Experiences of grief and loss are highly individualised. It is important to note that although the intensity of these reactions can be alarming, they can all be regarded as appropriate responses and are part of the natural healing process.

Resolving Grief

In many cases of relationship breakdown a number of people will be grieving and enduring the lack of balance and emotional ups and downs that go with that. The good news is that awareness is half the battle in putting people on course to a solution. In successful grief resolution, the goal is to re-establish emotional equilibrium. The main aspects necessary for successful grief resolution include:

- Accepting the reality of your loss.
- Experiencing the pain of your grief.
- Empathising with your partner.
- Adjusting to your new environment.
- Telling your story.
- Reinvesting your emotional energy.

Accepting

Acceptance is a key to moving through grief. This complex reaction involves a combination of factors. On the one hand, it involves recognising that life has changed, perhaps permanently and certainly for an extended period of time. It means letting go of your past life and also of the future as you envisioned it when you got married. At the same time, acceptance involves a willingness and even eagerness to build a new life. I call this combination 'acceptance with a fighting spirit'.

It can be difficult to accept the reality of your loss, since, unlike a death, in most instances it is ongoing and so there is no concrete focus for grief. There may also be no opportunity to experience the pain of the loss since emotions are often kept within in an attempt not to burden friends and family. Children especially can feel that expressing their true thoughts and feelings will make others uncomfortable and often do not verbalise their grief. Instead they often suppress and deny their pain – but like air bubbles in badly hung wallpaper, the pain reappears in other areas of their daily lives.

Couples counselling can be very useful in helping adults to recognise and accept that their relationship has ended and that separation is the best option for all concerned. If adults can agree and recognise this, children can, in turn, be clearly advised that while their parents will no longer be husband and wife they will always be Mammy and Daddy. The earlier a couple can accept their new reality, the easier the movement through grief for the entire family.

Some separating people place added blame on themselves for not being able to 'get over it'. If the person feels responsible for the loss, it results in even greater feelings of shame and guilt. If the separation is due to infidelity or addictive behaviours, the offending partner often feels to blame for the breakdown, making grief resolution even more difficult.

The effects of disenfranchised grief and consequent poor grief resolution are displayed in a variety of ways and to varying degrees. Depression, emotional disturbances, withdrawal from society, psychosomatic illnesses and low self-esteem are all common symptoms. A number of separating people succumb to substance abuse or damaging behaviours, while others have difficulty in forming healthy new relationships as they have not moved on from their broken relationship. The loss of community that may occur as a consequence of disenfranchised grief fosters an abiding sense of loneliness and abandonment, to the degree that the people involved often withdraw from their everyday activities and spend their time trying to battle negative thoughts. As difficult as it seems, the first steps are to recognise and accept if any of the above are occurring for you.

Experiencing
The key action in overcoming grief is to experience the pain of the loss and commence the grief work. One way to experience the pain is to look at any documentation that tells the story of the relationship, such as photographs and letters. This is a simple but effective way of acknowledging that the relationship was valid and based on love, but that over time you have grown apart and can no longer maintain an intimate relationship. It can be painful to look through such memories, but it is healthy as it allows each person to experience pain as opposed to ignoring it. This exercise can provide a major source of comfort – by remembering the good times people can accept the finality of loss. I have often observed this when working with people on group and individual programmes. In the words of one person, they are able to accept that their life has changed and they need to live differently, perhaps for the rest of their life. At the same time, however, they are able to keep a connection to positive aspects of their past. It also helped them to recognise some of their personality strengths, such as adaptability, determination and courage in adversity.

Empathising
The best indicator of whether a couple can separate whilst avoiding a messy battle is how much empathy they show for each other and for their children. It is the case with a large number of the couples I have worked with that

one partner experiences a greater sense of loss than the other. One particular client described the moment when it dawned on her that the relationship was dead as the 'gut-ripper of her life', following five years of bitter fighting. Very few separations are clean cut; most are based on a number of years of hostility, sadness, loneliness and desperate attempts to put the relationship back on track. The lonely path to relationship breakdown is very often scattered with losses and hardship, from constant arguing and infidelity to domestic violence and alcohol or drug addiction. Key to a successful separation is accepting the other person for who they are. Keep in mind that your partner may have been unprepared for the loss of the relationship. With this in mind, it is possible to have some empathy for their suffering. This merely means that where possible, you will give this person some breathing space as they accept that the relationship is over.

The special intimacy that couples share in the early years of their relationship contrasts sharply with the miserable years they may endure preceding their separation. In the past you may have been best friends, lovers and soulmates. Couples often describe the good times, when they felt they had a perfect partner – devoted, good-humoured, an excellent provider and so on. During separation, people often feel abandoned and, consequently, vulnerable and alone. A small amount of empathy can go a long way in avoiding angry battles, both emotional and legal.

Adjusting
An important way of overcoming grief is to adjust to your new environment. The role of support groups in this process cannot be overstated. To have other people validate your

pain and loss through experience and understanding is a very effective step towards healing. Many people who have not experienced relationship breakdown do not truly understand what is involved. While in general people will demonstrate care and compassion, very often a person who has experienced the reality of such loss offers better advice and support. I see this frequently in groups, when people say things like, 'It's so good to be with people who understand what I'm going through.'

People can question their ability to live a life beyond their relationship and to find another person they can love and trust. In a group they meet and hear from people who were in the same situation but are now living a new life with a loving partner, and who, in many cases, have a stronger relationship with their children than ever before.

Not many people want to talk about perceived failure, and men especially keep their pain to themselves. Although it may be buried, the emotional pain of loss often manifests itself in anger, fear, disappointment, vengeance, punishment, guilt and deep sorrow. The key is to understand that all these emotions are normal and are there to be experienced. This is all part of your mind's attempt to adjust to your new life. This is a temporary part of the process and it is during this time that you need to find caring, compassionate people to whom you can speak.

It is important to understand that there are several common responses to the losses brought by a relationship breakdown. For most people, there is not a neat, orderly progression. Rather, grief is an individual process, in which a person may experience some but not necessarily all of the emotions described above. Also, a person may experience some emotions more than once, or may feel two or more at the same time. Many clients have described the experience as like being tossed about in a whirlpool of grief.

Deciding to separate may produce relief, because you have finally made a decision. Yet this initial reaction is often accompanied by shock and disbelief. Denial can be an adaptive response, allowing gradual adjustment to all the changes in your life and to the uncertainty brought about by a separation. Denial is a way to keep hope alive when life has been turned upside down, but if you get stuck in this phase it is impossible to face your situation realistically. It often leads to repeated unsuccessful attempts at reconciliation, which may reinforce a sense of helplessness and despair.

Anger, frustration, rage and envy are the most common reactions I hear from individuals in the counselling room. These are genuine emotions that honour and recognise change and uncertainty. Feeling angry is normal and can have positive effects if it motivates you to action; but anger can be destructive if it is expressed in a way that drives away people who want to help. Expressing anger by shouting or by being cruel is hurtful and generally makes the situation worse.

Some people blame themselves for the breakdown of their relationship: 'If only I had taken better care of myself' or 'If only I had paid better attention to my spouse.' Guilt can be helpful if it motivates you to take better care of yourself from here forward, but it can be a trap if you see your life and current relationships as a personal failure. Whatever happened before, you can only exercise control from here on.

Depression and feelings of sadness are common during and post separation or divorce. Depression may also be triggered by a long period of suffering before deciding to separate. Usually depression eases over time. If it lasts, you will have a sense of despair and inertia. Several strategies may be helpful, depending on the degree of depression: use self-help techniques to confirm that all that could have been done was done to save the relationship; work to change your thinking so that it is more realistic and helpful – counselling and particularly cognitive behavioural therapy (CBT) can help; if you have reached the stage where you are unable to think or act then you may be suffering from clinical depression and should seek professional medical guidance and possibly medication – it is important not to self-medicate with drugs or alcohol.

Telling

Relationship breakdown can be a major trauma. When someone suffers a trauma, part of their recovery is telling their story. The accident victim will go over and over the story – 'I looked away for a matter of seconds. Why didn't I keep my eyes on the road?' – trying to understand what happened. Psychologically, the person is reworking and retelling the story until it no longer creates unmanageable levels of emotional stress. In the course of a relationship breakdown, it is imperative that you find space to tell your story. This might take the form of writing it down and reading it from time to time, or simply by talking to a friend or counsellor. This will take some of the negative energy from the story, give the mind a rest and create space for the positive aspects of your life.

While some separated people are resilient and bounce back in their own time, some can get stuck in grief, and those people may be helped by therapy. This counselling may involve telling their story of loss, with the therapist sometimes helping reframe the experience in a more positive way. A therapist can also help the person to develop new goals and re-engage with life. Good counselling can help a person to come out the other side of grief, to accept their new life and even become energised by the new opportunities the separation has presented to them.

Reinvesting
In time you will begin to move on with your life. This can be aided by engaging in new activities and relationships, by putting your emotional energy into tasks that encourage you to live. It is also important to understand that the task remains of emotionally withdrawing from your former partner and of recasting them in a new role in your life. One needs to be careful in doing this, so as not to emotionally withdraw from your children as well. In fact, it may be good to take some of the emotional energy you invested in your former partner and instead invest this in your children. Remember the breakdown is between two adults, and that the decision is to stop being husband and wife. The roles of father and mother remain unchanged, and, if anything, need to become stronger to ensure your children receive extra attention at this time of transition.

As you accept and negotiate each stage you will gain strength, until you have successfully completed the process. However, keep in mind that this will not restore you to a pre-grief separation state. The experience will change you, and in accepting this you can move on with your life while thinking of your broken relationship in a healthy way.

Practical Strategies

Grief does not abate, but changes over time. It will go from a sharp pang to a dull thud and eventually fades from being the primary concern in your life. A simple but practical way to understand grief is to imagine your mind as being similar to the old-fashioned pistons of a steam train: one of the pistons is 'loss orientated' and the other is 'restoration orientated'. Loss orientation is where we tend to focus on the past and how much we will miss what went before. It includes all the strong emotions and sad thoughts. Restoration orientation concerns the practicalities of life, distraction from grief and exploration of future possibilities. While such practical and necessary tasks are being addressed, grief has to be sidelined. Your mind needs to expect and also ensure both pistons are working and that there is an oscillation between concentrating on recovery and also giving time to think about and accept the loss. In other words, by fluctuating between the two processes, you will obtain the benefits of each – exploring the loss and coping with daily life.

There are several social features associated with a positive response to loss, and people who cope well often have a number of factors in their favour, such as better than average finances, a decent level of education, fewer stressors and good health. Yet there are many factors that aid in positive adjustment to loss that all of us can learn and practise; for example, avoiding rumination on your loss and accepting the need for flexibility and optimism. Limiting rumination means learning to shift attention away from grief at times when thinking about loss is no longer productive; flexibility means the ability to adjust coping strategies to different situations; and optimism involves the conviction that things will turn out for the best in the end. Resilient people are able to see benefits even of their negative experiences. Those who have been through a separation often say, 'I never knew I could be so strong' or 'my loss helped me focus on what is really important.' They acknowledge their loss but also say things like, 'The new me is a kinder, gentler and more caring person.'

The pervasiveness of loss presents us with one of our biggest tasks: bringing meaning to life when so much has been taken away. Below are a number of practical strategies for moving through the inevitable grief:

Use problem-solving: One way to move through grief is to use its emotions as the impetus to adopt self-management strategies to remedy the situations that triggered the emotions.

Keep structure in your life: Having a routine provides a sense of stability and familiarity, counteracting the feelings of disorientation and uncertainty brought about by the changes in your family life. Do not make any unnecessary major changes in your life during times of loss, as they can further add to the existing instability and anxiety.

Avoid unnecessary stress: Adjusting to the many changes brought about by the end of a relationship can be hard and even traumatic. When you are already overloaded emotionally it is best to avoid people and situations that add to that stress.

Respond positively to self-pity: Everyone involved in a relationship breakdown feels sorry for themselves occasionally. It is not unusual to feel overwhelmed by emotions, given the loss and stress experienced. Acknowledging self-pity can take some of its power away. You might say something like, 'I'm feeling sorry for myself.' It can also help to console yourself with thoughts like, 'I've felt this way before and it has always blown over, so it won't last this time either.'

Rest: Strong emotions can be triggered and exacerbated by fatigue. Rest may help alleviate both physical and emotional symptoms.

Connect with others: Reach out via phone, email or in person. Sometimes just being in touch with others can change a mood. At other times it helps to have your mood acknowledged.

Help others: Shift attention away from yourself and on to what you can do for your family, friends or others in your life.

Spiritual and Social Connection

Often it is through our experience of pain and sorrow that we build hope for a better future and come to recognise the beauty of things we often take for granted. Individuals who have been through a contentious relationship breakdown often think of themselves in negative terms that can, for some, become self-fulfilling prophecies. Clients I have worked with who have experienced an acrimonious break-up often convey that they feel worthless and emptied. As one client put it, 'It is as if I've fallen into a bottomless pit.'

Participation in spiritual rituals can give a person a sense of being loved and valued exactly as they are. Spiritual activity, either at a personal level or as part of a religious community, helps individuals engage in non-negative thinking and instead develop a coherent worldview and approach to life, based on love and compassion rather than hate and anger. Spiritually-based activities help to:

- Normalise reactions and internal struggles.
- Encourage emotional expression, emotional control and emotional comfort.
- Foster recognition and self-acceptance.
- Highlight the benefits of opening up and sharing.

The key mechanisms are:

- Contemplation, meditation and mindfulness activities that can reduce anxiety.
- Acceptance and forgiveness activities that control negative emotions like anger, guilt and shame, as well as nurture empathy.
- Community support and sharing.
- Faith and prayer.

These mechanisms convey a sense of connection and control that helps people feel they are not mere victims of arbitrary events and to move away from the sense that bad things happen to good people or that good things happen to bad people. They also foster social connectedness with like-minded people. By sharing one's story with others who face a similar situation, one has the opportunity to see that lessons, insight and even blessings can come from hardship and adversity.

Sociality, spirituality and meaning-making are central features of human beings and the relational and collective connectedness help combat feelings of isolation and loneliness and can be very beneficial to the healing process. Socially connected individuals are more likely to meet the demands of everyday stressors by means of active coping and by recruiting help from others. They are more likely to behave in a selfless fashion, reinforcing their connections to others and enhancing their self-esteem at this time of immense change.

Avoiding Messy Court Cases

During separation and divorce it is important to make fair, balanced and rational decisions that meet the needs of all parties. Dealing with relationship breakdown within the court system can take an extremely long time, during which physical and emotional health are often sacrificed. The somewhat adversarial approach taken by the legal system can leave families and individuals feeling bruised, while the large fees commanded can render them financially ill-prepared for the future.

Alternative dispute resolution (ADR) is a term used to describe the options that aid people to settle civil disputes without the need for a formal court hearing. It is about getting both sides to collaborate by listening to each other and agreeing on a mutually beneficial solution prior to entering the legal system. Although it is mainly used in consumer and commercial disputes, over the last decade interest in ADR has steadily been growing in the area of relationship breakdown and family law cases. It now provides realistic ways of resolving disputes other than acrimonious and costly court proceedings.

These collaborative methods can help separating couples to work through their emotions and also make informed choices as to the best future options for all involved. The various approaches are not intended to replace the courts but they can have advantages over a court-only approach. They are more person centred, flexible, less stressful and less expensive. The ADR approach also promotes a faster and longer-lasting resolution to relationship breakdown. It may also help ensure that you engage in better communication with your former partner in the future. There are a number of alternatives available to separating couples.

Relationship Counselling

Relationship counselling attempts to create a safe space in which couples can resolve problems in their relationship or to improve their relationship to ease the path through separation. Typically, both people attend counselling sessions together to discuss specific issues, although it is also possible for an individual at the end of a relationship to attend alone. Research shows that individuals and their problems are best handled within the context of their relationships and that counselling, when effective, tends to improve a person's physical as well as mental health, in addition to improving their relationships with others. Relationship counselling helps couples learn to deal more effectively with problems, and can help prevent small issues from escalating out of control.

Most counsellors are trained in psychotherapy and family systems, and focus on understanding their clients' symptoms and the way their interactions contribute to problems in the relationship. It is usually a short-term solution-focused therapy ranging from four to twelve sessions. It is common practice for counsellors to ask questions about the couple's roles, patterns, rules, goals and beliefs. Therapy often begins with the couple reflecting on both the good and bad aspects of their relationship. The counsellor then works with the couple to help them understand that, in most cases, both partners are contributing to problems in the relationship. When this is understood, the couple learns to change how they interact with each other, and improved communication is often the result. The partners may be encouraged to draw up a contract in which each describes the behaviour he or she will try to maintain.

A lot of couples assume that marriage and relationship counselling is all about keeping a couple together. However, this is not always the case. Effective counselling facilitates couples in exploring, reflecting upon and resolving difficulties in their relationship. The resolution may in fact be the decision to separate on a trial basis, to separate permanently or to divorce. For many years I have worked with separating couples to provide a safe, confidential space in which they can agree on how to end the relationship and consider the options available to them. The aim is to ensure the best approach for individuals and the entire family. Whatever the outcome, it is the separating couple that decides the way forward.

Couples with children may also seek post-marital therapy for help in working out their differences. Couples in this situation can find that marriage therapy during separation can help them find a common ground as they negotiate interpersonal, financial and childcare issues.

Family Mediation
Mediation is now widely recognised throughout the western world as the most popular form of alternative dispute resolution. Mediation helps those involved in relationship breakdown to communicate better with one another and reach their own decisions about children, property and

finances, as well as offering a cost-effective alternative to court proceedings. Family mediation is based on the same principles that apply in mediation generally; that is, participation is voluntary. This ensures both separating adults have a commitment to the process. It is open and transparent, which is essential when working with couples that may be experiencing a lack of trust. The process is based on mutual respect, which facilitates the separating couple to engage in productive behaviours. Mediation is not marriage counselling or a legal advice service. However, it allows people to make their own decisions and hold on to their own power during a time of immense change.

Mediation has a structure and dynamic that ordinary negotiation lacks. The process usually takes between three and six one-hour sessions and is private and confidential. It involves both people meeting in a neutral place with an independent mediator. Mediators use various techniques to open or improve dialogue between separating couples, aiming to help the parties reach an agreement on the best way forward for their family. The mediator's role is to create a climate of co-operation and responsibility, in which neither party dominates and both parties participate fully in good faith. This process helps both clients to deal with the difficult emotional issues that can prevent them reaching agreement, and the final result is to reach a solution they both find acceptable. For successful mediation to begin the separating couple must agree and understand that:

- Both parties must attend.
- Discussions are confidential.
- The mediator is impartial.

The main advantages being:

- It is a confidential service.
- A balanced agreement is reached that is acceptable to the parties.
- Decisions taken together are more likely to be honoured.
- It promotes communication and co-operation, reducing bitterness and distress.
- Parents are helped to remain as partners in child-rearing by developing parenting plans that suit their particular circumstances.
- Parents are helped to manage conflict in a way that protects the best interests of their children.
- The service is free in many countries and is a lot less costly than a solicitor.

Family mediation encourages the separating couple to co-operate with each other in working out mutually acceptable arrangements regarding child custody and access, guardianship, legal separation, sibling disputes, child maintenance, spousal maintenance, and disputes regarding inheritances, amongst other matters.

The mediator examines the dispute and strips it down to its bare bones. They then examine how the dispute escalated. In doing so they have regard for all the different components of a dispute, the power balance between the parties, communication issues, financial issues, positions and persuasiveness. With this information in place, the mediator can lead the parties to a path of communication that directs them towards a successful resolution. Mediations can either take place with everyone in the same room, or the two sides to the dispute in separate rooms. Co-mediation uses a male and female mediator to deal with male and female clients respectively, as some clients find that this provides better balance.

At the outset of the process, mediators ask parties to examine their needs and wants and to reflect on the envisaged outcome. More importantly, they ask people to consider alternatives that might resolve the dispute. The process starts with both sides getting a chance to read a short opening statement to the other side. Although this statement is generally only a few lines in length, it can be as long as the parties wish. It is not an opportunity to take potshots at each other, but rather an opportunity for each person to state why they are attending mediation and what they hope to achieve. Parties generally reflect at this time on their desire for resolution for themselves and particularly on the needs of any children that might be involved.

The earlier part of separation mediation generally deals with the financial aspects of the dispute: both sides make a financial declaration in a financial summary document. The mediators then assist the parties in organising their paperwork. Generally, this involves recent wage slips, annual accounts, bank statements, credit card statements and any other documents used to vouch for financial circumstances. On average, this can take two sessions. Parties generally find this part of the process useful as it allows them to focus on their daily spending and on bills. (People are often shocked by how much they are spending.) The information and research gained from this part of the process can assist a separating couple at the later stages of the mediation when future financial arrangements are discussed.

As stated earlier, mediation is a key alternative dispute resolution service, and while there may be no obligation to attend mediation, in many cases any settlement agreement signed by the parties forms the basis of a binding legal agreement. The independent mediator assists the couple in negotiating their own settlement and can help form a view on what might be fair or reasonable. They also prepare the documentation for the basis of any legally binding orders. Most mediations end with a written document that sets out all the details of the couple's agreement. This can then be taken to solicitors to be drawn into a legal contract and/or used as the basis for a court order. When a couple have reached agreement, a session can very often be offered to parents with children to discuss their new family arrangements in an encouraging and positive way.

The disputants decide the terms of the agreement, not the mediator. However, the mediator has an extremely important role in 'reality testing' any agreement. This means that they have to check carefully whether or not the parties are actually able to do what they have agreed to do, so that the agreement has a chance to survive in the reality of separation and divorce.

In the throes of separation, people have a tendency to issue the other side with ultimatums. Mediation teaches couples to switch off threatening language and approach the situation with a problem-solving attitude. The tools learned by clients in mediation serve them well in other types of disputes they encounter in life.

Neil and Dawn

Neil and Dawn had been married for six years and had two small children aged four and six. They had decided to separate but were not ready to think about divorce just yet. Neil agreed that he would move out of the family home, but prior to this they needed to work out their finances, both short- and long-term. Both Neil and Dawn worked at the time. Both parties wanted to use mediation to make decisions about their finances and to try to avoid resorting to the courts.

Mediation began with the couple putting together an agenda of what they needed to address. It was clear that the first point that needed to be dealt with was the short-term finances, which would allow Neil to move out and rent a flat. They brought together all their financial information and went through it with the mediator. They managed to work out that Neil could rent a two-bedroom flat near to the family home. However, they would need to use some of their joint savings to pay for this. It was agreed that this should continue for six months, after which time bigger decisions would need to be taken about the family home and the other aspects of their financial situation. Once they had agreed the short-term arrangements, the mediator helped them to put together a list of decisions that would need to be taken within the next six months, including what they wanted to do about their marriage in the legal sense.

The children did not yet know about the separation, so they discussed how they were going to tell them. The mediator helped them to agree a 'script', where neither parent blamed the other but would not give the children any false expectations. The couple talked about how often the children would see their father. They had originally thought that Neil could see the children whenever he wanted to, but in the course of mediation they agreed that a pre-arranged routine would be better for everyone.

Once these short-term issues were resolved, the couple left mediation, but they returned four months later as they had decided to proceed with a divorce. With the help of the mediator they finalised an agreed approach to their finances and each took away an orderly file, together with a summary of their proposals, to give to their respective solicitors.

Collaborative Law

Collaborative law is non-confrontational and progressive in nature. It encourages parties to focus on the future and problem-solving strategies rather than the problems of the past. The system is also child-centred and the parties are encouraged to make special provision for the needs of children. Since its inception in the 1980s, the collaborative law movement has spread rapidly to most of the United States, Europe, Canada and Australia and more than 22,000 lawyers and solicitors have been trained in collaborative law worldwide. The growth of the collaborative process has been encouraged by both the judiciary and family law organisations as a response to the spiralling cost of relationship breakdown. (The collaborative process can be used to facilitate a broad range of family issues beyond relationship breakdown, including disputes between parents and the drawing up of pre- and post-marital contracts. The traditional method of drawing up pre-marital contracts is oppositional, and many couples prefer to begin their married life on a better footing by drawing up documents consensually.)

Collaborative law has a distinct advantage, in that it is a legal process enabling separating couples to work with their respective lawyers – and, on occasion, other family professionals – in order to achieve a settlement that best meets the specific needs of both parties and their children without the underlying threat of contested litigation. Collaborative law differs from mediation in that each of the parties is represented by their solicitor. Both parties to the dispute retain separate, specifically trained solicitors whose only task is to help them with their disagreements. The voluntary process is initiated when the couple signs a contract (called the 'participation agreement'), binding them to the process. Each of the separating parties must have a solicitor who is committed to the ideals of collaborative law. The separating parties are at the centre of the process and actively involved in the negotiation, which is an empowering process.

Negotiations take place in a number of four-way settlement meetings attended by both clients and solicitors. The number of meetings required differs with each couple, depending on the complexity of the issues involved. The agenda for each meeting is agreed between the clients and solicitors beforehand. The purpose of the four-way meeting is to reach a settlement, which is negotiated by both clients directly, while the solicitors provide legal advice if needed.

Each solicitor is there to ensure that their client is guided towards a reasonable resolution, that the process is a fair one, that the negotiations are conducted in a non-contentious environment, that full financial disclosure has been made by both parties and that any additional expert opinion required in relation to financial issues can be agreed and shared between the parties. (If financial, medical or other experts are required, then one expert is retained to advise both parties, as opposed to the traditional litigation approach of retaining separate experts to advise each client.)

In the event that the collaborative law process does not work, perhaps due to a lack of trust or because the parties are unable to reach agreement, neither solicitor can continue to act for their client in any future contentious litigation between the parties. This is enshrined in the collaborative law process signed by the parties and their respective solicitors. Collaborative law is not suited to all couples; a degree of trust is necessary and they must have a reasonably amicable relationship.

Sarah and Ray

Sarah and Ray, the parents of two children, were married for ten years when Ray told Sarah he was having an affair and wanted a divorce. He moved out and then moved back in as they tried relationship counselling. Eventually they agreed the marriage wasn't going to survive. Both were apprehensive about the future. Specifically, they worried if they would have enough money to live comfortably and support their children's needs and were determined that the divorce would not affect their children emotionally. They had seen divorcing friends squander their life-savings fighting each other in court and agreed that this was not the right approach for them.

A counsellor suggested mediation. However, Sarah felt she needed to be represented by her own solicitor as Ray had knowledge about finances which she felt put her at a disadvantage. As Sarah wasn't working and one child wasn't yet in school, she needed to ensure any agreement

Brainse Rátheanaigh
Raheny Branch
Tel: 8315521

secured immediate financial support. She was also very angry and wanted to ensure that she had a good team behind her at this vulnerable time in her life. A friend facilitated Sarah and Ray in making contact with two solicitors experienced in collaborative law. The solicitors guided the couple in defining their goals and priorities.

An accountant and a counsellor completed the collaborative team. The accountant gathered information on their spending habits and suggested various financial scenarios to meet their goals. The counsellor, whose role was to prioritise the welfare of the children, met privately with Sarah and then with Ray. Beyond discussing their issues and concerns, the counsellor identified behaviours that triggered each other's negative reactions and worked with them to ensure their emotions would not undermine the collaborative approach. The counsellor also talked with the children and reported back to the parents and the team. A parenting plan was developed and both children's feelings and concerns were incorporated into the divorce resolution.

When the team met, the counsellor helped Sarah and Ray set ground rules to ensure civil, respectful communications. However, some meetings were still heated, as Sarah blamed Ray for destroying the family. The counsellor helped Ray understand that Sarah needed time to adjust to her new situation.

By the end of the process, Sarah and Ray had constructed a mutually beneficial agreement that was very different from the terms of a typical adversarial separation and divorce case. They were happy because they crafted it together, addressing the whole family's needs and priorities.

Three years later, the children are doing well in school and enjoy good relationships with both parents. The co-parenting transition from one household to the other was seamless. Neither parent undermines the other and both Sarah and Ray are actively involved in their children's lives and care about what is important to them.

The collaborative law approach helped this family navigate complex legal, emotional and financial issues, along with a new style of handling conflict that continues to work well today.

Trial Separation

Before deciding on full legal separation or divorce it is worth discussing the option of a trial separation. Many couples reach a point in their relationship where they are disillusioned. For these people, respite from the marital relationship may allow them to deal with the crisis before they are confronted with mending or ending the marriage. Personal space can provide individuals with much greater clarity on who they are and whether they want to continue to share their life with their current partner. However, this type of separation needs careful consideration, as in some cases it may mark the end of a marriage.

Over the years the main circumstances from which couples have initiated a trial separation are:

- Both partners recognise that the frequency, intensity and duration of their disagreement has become overwhelming.
- The couple acknowledge that for a long time there has been a lack of positive interaction and agree to a separation in the hope of raising levels of mutual positive exchange.

- Both partners realise that they need more personal and emotional space or an opportunity for personal growth and individual freedom while restructuring the relationship or considering the best way forward for the entire family.

Trial separation is often misunderstood due to the lack of guidelines and the ease with which it can be carried out. It can be fraught with many pitfalls if clear objectives are not put in place. It is best defined as a time-limited approach in which the couple terminate cohabitation, commit to regularly scheduled therapy with a therapist and agree to regular interpersonal contact without deciding whether to reunite or not. The most basic goal of any trial separation is to give the couple space and time to decide on future action, without undue influence from each other. The options following a trial separation are simply to mend it or to end it. Either way a space has been created for each individual to reflect.

A pitfall of a trial separation can be that once separated, some people will see the break as an opportunity for them to start new relationships. This complicates the situation and makes finding a solution to the marital problems much harder. Another pitfall is that one partner might take advantage of the situation and not allow the other partner back into the family home.

In order to make a trial separation successful, a couple should agree to four key rules:

Determine a time frame
The break should have a specific time attached to it, so that it does not drag on without conclusion. The time should

ideally be between three and six months, so that a sense of urgency is retained, especially where children are involved. The longer the separation continues and people settle into a new routine, the harder it is to get back to the old life.

Set clear boundaries

It is important to know the rules of the separation – what is acceptable and what isn't. Work these rules out with a counsellor and stick to them.

Remain committed to marriage/relationship therapy

There should be communication between the couple, with regular times to meet with a counsellor to reflect on whether the relationship deserves another chance or if the time has come to move on. Trial separation also allows individuals to step back from what has gone before and to try to understand the other person and their concerns. If the other person is doing the same, a better understanding of the underlying problems and how they can be resolved is likely to be reached with much less acrimony.

Plan for financial obligations and childcare

There should be clear agreement about what happens to the finances during a separation, with equal sharing of resources and children adequately taken care of. Running two households is likely to be more expensive. This should be settled before the separation takes place, so that no one person bears the brunt of any financial or care burden that might ensue.

James and Deirdre

During the course of couples therapy, hostility between James and Deirdre reached a peak. They stormed out of the session, screaming at each other and swearing vengeance in the divorce courts. Both contacted the therapist separately later in the week, apologising for their behaviour and asking if they could attend another session. The therapist told them that they needed to agree as a couple and to come back when they were both ready.

One month later, they arrived back in the therapist's office. Even though their problems remained, they were more respectful of each other during the session. They explained that following the last session they had decided to live in separate houses (they were lucky enough to have a second property near to the family home). During the separation, and under the sincere conviction that the relationship was over, they somehow began to act differently towards each other. They realised that to help their two small children they had to collaborate; that it was not in their interests to be aggressive and fight. Most importantly, they realised that they had been taking each other for granted. Each had stopped seeing their spouse as a real person and they had lost the connection that every couple requires: the connection of friendship.

Grandparents

Understandably, most of the literature on the impact of relationship breakdown focuses on the separating couple and their children. However, the potential contribution of grandparents should not be overlooked and deserves attention in its own right. The shape of families is shifting from horizontal to vertical. Today, many young people reach adulthood with several grandparents still around; and at the same time, decreases in family size means that grandparents have fewer grandchildren. In many cases, grandparenthood is likely to last for several decades, with the relationships being more intimate. As such, grandparents are generally key influencers in many families.

The Importance of Grandparents
When couples first marry, grandparents can provide a safe foundation from which new parents and their young children can negotiate the challenges of modern life. Grandparents can support both adults and children during this time of development and change as they grow together as a young family. One of the most noticeable points raised by clients is that the quality of the grandparent–grandchild relationship is different to that of the parent–child experience. Adult children often remark on how their parents are much more

flexible and forgiving when dealing with their grandchildren than they were with them as children. Grandparents I have spoken to affirm this and ascribe it to three factors: they know that they only have a certain amount of time with their grandchildren and they want to use that time to show their love and affection; they have learned from the past and have become more patient and understanding, learning to react better when things go wrong; they have more spare time and so are less prone to stress, unlike when they were busy, working parents.

Grandparents have more time to listen on a one-to-one basis than most of the other trusted adults a child will encounter. In a busy world, grandparents are a haven, providing warm, relaxed care. However, the grandparent–grandchild relationship is contingent on several factors and these key variables are thought to influence the frequency of contact and the quality of the relationship if a marriage ends.

Research indicates that regardless of the frequency of interaction, grandmothers appear to derive a greater satisfaction from their role than grandfathers.[2] Grandmothers mention more frequently a desire to act as a source of wisdom and knowledge to their grandchildren, while grandfathers believe they can be more useful in providing support to their own sons and daughters. Grandfathers felt that other roles – including those of a husband, father, worker and participant in social and leisure clubs – were as important as grandparenthood. There is also evidence to suggest that grandfathers living alone, either as a result of being widowed, separated or divorced, interact with their

---

2. K. Somary, and G. Stricker, 'Becoming a Grandparent: A Longitudinal Study of Expectations and Early Experiences as a Function of Sex and Lineage', *Gerontologist* 38.1 (1998): 53–61.

grandchildren less frequently than grandfathers living with their spouse.

Geographical proximity also influences the closeness of the grandparent–grandchild relationship, affecting the frequency of face-to-face contact and the ability of grandparents to be involved in the lives of their grandchildren. Routine involvement in everyday activities and networks helps to develop strong bonds between grandparents and grandchildren. Contact is an important influence on the relationship. Today, however, geographical distance does not inevitably compromise psychological closeness to grandchildren, and the importance of Skype, telephone and email contact cannot be underestimated.

The age of both the grandparent and grandchild can also influence the quality of the relationship. Emotional intimacy is not constant and generally older grandparents intimate higher levels of affection with their grandchildren than younger grandparents. As a grandchild enters adolescence, the nature of the relationship becomes more voluntary and is often characterised by deeper communication, mutual exchange, guidance and support. While the onset of adolescence may put more stress on the parent–child relationship, it can be the opposite for the grandparent–grandchild relationship.[3]

It is the parents who bring the children to the grandparents and thus decide the frequency of contact. The power of the parents is so great in this regard that the relationship between younger children and their grandparents has been described as an indirect relationship that can only occur through the mediating influence of the

3. P. Uhlenberg and B. G. Hammill, 'Frequency of Grandparent Contact with Grandchild Sets: Six Factors that Make a Difference', *The Gerontologist* 38.3 (1998): 276–85.

children's parents. It is only when the grandchildren reach adulthood that the grandchildren–grandparent relationship is not mediated through the middle generation. Studies of grandparents note a phenomenon called the 'matrifocal tilt', where it is apparent that maternal grandmothers and grandchildren get to spend most time together and have the closest relationships.

While grandmothers, in the normal course of events, have more contact with grandchildren than grandfathers, some research has suggested that male and female grandchildren tend to interact more with grandparents of the same sex during a crisis. In reality, grandparents provide a great deal of emotional and practical support to their children and grandchildren and, as a consequence, they usually play an intimate role during the relationship breakdown process.

A final point worth noting is that grandparents today are younger. Many of the clients who arrive at my clinic are grandparents between the ages of fifty-five and sixty-five who are physically healthy and active but may be struggling psychologically to cope with the array of issues they are encountering at this point in their life. Very often the relationship breakdown of an adult child may be accompanied by retirement issues, health issues or the recent deaths of their own parents or friends.

The Grandparent–Grandchild Relationship After Separation

When love breaks down, grandparents can provide continuity and support to children in a way that few other trusted adults can. Depending on the existing level of contact, many grandparents find themselves taking on more responsibility for their grandchildren, while others experience a reduction in the amount of contact they have with their grandchildren. In instances where relationships between the adult generations remain intact or at least functional, grandparents have the potential to act as an important resource and can assist the parental generation by providing economic assistance, support or childcare.

Particularly in the early stages of the separation, grandparents who have had close relationships with their grandchildren have the opportunity to play a pivotal role in minimising disruption and helping to mitigate some of the distress or feelings of insecurity that a grandchild may experience. I have worked with separating families where grandparents were cognisant of the unsettling life event their grandchildren were negotiating. As such, they concentrated on providing continuity and reassurance to the children. Sensitive to the needs of their grandchildren, they treated them as a central concern and made themselves available as counsellors and confidants. They tried to normalise the situation for their grandchild and to distract and reassure them when necessary. They were anchors of stability at a time of uncertainty.

Grandparents often go to considerable lengths to reorganise their lives to accommodate the needs of their grandchildren following separation. In addition to providing practical hands-on care, grandparents can provide intellectual stimulation, emotional support, guidance and supervision. However, as time passes and the emotional turmoil that surrounds the relationship breakdown subsides, most grandparents are able to reduce the intensity of their involvement.

Sometimes the ending of a relationship can be so acrimonious that not only do children have reduced contact with their non-resident parent, but contact is also severed with that parent's family. Grandparents needlessly lose out in this situation, but it is the children who suffer the most. No good parent sets out to intentionally harm their child, but in the emotional turmoil of relationship breakdown it is surprisingly easy to make decisions that have a negative impact on children, such as withholding contact with grandparents. To avoid this situation it is important that both parents keep in mind that time spent with grandparents can be invaluable at this time. Grandparents can often help to defuse anger and hostility and make bewildered children feel loved and secure. When children's lives are disrupted they need a safe place to express feelings, emotional support and practical help. Children who are denied the right to see their grandparents often speak of this void during therapy. They miss the relationship and the little extras that grandparents can provide.

Grandparents who lose contact with their grandchildren can suffer from many negative long-term effects as a result of the difficulty of finding closure in the grieving process. Many can struggle to cope with the loss, and appear unable to think of little else. Clients I work with often remark that it has impinged upon their ability to love and trust others. One grandmother stated that she was reluctant to develop a close relationship with her second grandchild following the loss of contact with her first. This loss of contact with grandchildren is acutely felt and can result in anxiety and restlessness and can appear to be coupled with feelings of guilt, as well as concern over the well-being of their grandchildren.

It is important to keep in mind that the majority of children are highly resilient. Despite the complexities and insecurities of the situation, most grandparent–grandchild relationships remain intact and well-functioning. In some instances, the bond becomes closer due to co-residence or reduced contact with the non-custodial parent whose involvement had previously, to varying extents, marred the grandparent–grandchild relationship.

While new reforms throughout the western world have recognised the importance in a child's life of significant other people apart from their biological parents, courts are still concerned primarily with what is in the child's best interests, and are unwilling to expose them to unacceptable risk. Often during this time parents fail to recognise the value grandparents can be in their child's life. Conflict can be one of the most emotionally damaging things for children, and I would urge grandparents to give consideration to whether seeking to maintain a relationship with grandchildren, amidst severe opposition, will ultimately be in the child's best interests.

However, the key message is that grandparents can have a very valuable and worthwhile input into their grandchildren's lives. Except when it would be contrary to their best interests, children have a right of contact, on a regular basis, with both their parents and with other people significant to their care, welfare and development.

Grandparents Are Parents Too

Understandably, grandparents become deeply involved in their children's lives. Increased closeness is often the result of such emotional involvement. The breakdown of an adult child's relationship can mean changing plans such as holidays and family visits. It is important to reflect on reality and to plan for reconstituted family activities as far as possible. In some cases, adult children can become reliant on their parents during and following separation, forcing grandparents to revert to their earlier role of provider and protector, while their adult child can revert to being a dependent. This is most likely when an adult child moves back in with them on a temporary or sometimes long-term basis.

The role of grandparents in companioning their adult children through the separation or divorce process is considerable, and in close-knit families can be the lynchpin to the younger generation's ability to negotiate the emotional and practical fallout from a relationship breakdown. The wisdom of an older, more experienced person is particularly important. When all are losing their heads and blaming each other, grandparents can help to maintain family relationships, offer stability, listen to their adult children and offer respite from the turmoil.

Relationships with a son or daughter's former partner tend to be complex and, if not well managed, can be characterised by animosity. A number of grandparents also grieve for the positive relationship they had with their child's former partner. All the adults involved need to renegotiate their roles carefully. If everyone can accept the new reality of the situation, the relationships can be of a broadly positive character, particularly after the period of initial conflict has come to an end.

Some grandparents experience a great deal of anger during the separation process. This can be exacerbated by the lack of support available to help them cope and provide support to others. Such anger is most often expressed in situations where divorce or custody proceedings are still underway, and the final potential impact on all is still unknown. Where expressed, the anger is most often targeted at their child's former partner, whom they may hold responsible for the relationship breakdown and the hurt caused. This anger is often related to changed expectations about their child's and grandchildren's future and may have been simply a way of expressing emotion over their personal disappointment and concerns over the well-being of their family.

When providing support to their children, grandparents must be careful not to neglect their own needs or take on too much stress and responsibility. To do this, grandparents must sort through their own thoughts and emotions. They need to accept, recognise and process any thoughts and feelings of confusion, sadness, anger and fear. It is important that grandparents take some time to do their own grieving in private, as this can help them to accept the situation. This time can also help them ensure that they do not take sides, offer unwanted advice or tell their already burdened adult child how upset or disappointed they are.

Many grandparents think that it is better to provide support first and only think about themselves after the needs of others have been met. Research shows this is not the best approach. Grandparents will not be a source of strength and support for their own child and grandchildren until they have addressed their own emotions and thoughts on the matter. As they say on flights, 'Put on your own oxygen mask before attending to your children.'

Remember that Grandparents Are Also Suffering

Each grandparent will have their own unique emotional journey as they seek to come to terms with their child's relationship breakdown. This is influenced by a variety of factors, which include those that grandparents have some control over and those they are not in a position to control. Personal impact on the grandparent is highly dependent on the degree of acrimony in the relationship breakdown. Concern for the well-being of an adult child and grandchildren are the main reasons for the shared negative impact on both grandparents.

Once the separation process begins, many grandparents also experience feelings of apprehension because of uncertainty over the outcome of the process. The power is in the hands of the separating couple to make their own arrangements with regards to custody and, as a result, grandparents can feel helpless.

It is important for grandparents to access support where they can in order to discuss their thoughts and feelings and learn to accept that their children and grandchildren's life will be drastically changed. There is very little formal support available to guide the majority of grandparents through the process of their child's separation, with many formal support services focused on the separating adults and their children. However, many use informal support from family and friends, the benefits of which should not be underestimated. It can provide an opportunity to work through grief and anger, and also in some cases enable one to see the point of view of a child's former spouse or partner, which in turn allows one to provide one's own child and other family members with support. It is also worth recognising that most relationship counselling services will help grandparents to discuss their thoughts and emotions and support them through the separation.

Paula

Paula was a sixty-seven-year-old grandmother whose son had moved back in with her following his separation from his wife over one year previously. The separation was in some way a relief to Paula and her husband, as her son and daughter-in-law had a volatile relationship, which had caused suffering for all involved.

Paula spoke of how much free time she had now she was retired, but was disappointed how little time she now spent with her grandchildren. She was aware, however, that their maternal grandmother was seeing a lot of them. Paula described how her contact with her grandchildren, which had included regular child-minding, changed abruptly when her son separated and moved back into her house. He continued to fight with his wife and this often resulted in her suddenly deciding that he wasn't allowed to see the children. When her son had asked his wife if Paula could see the children, her daughter-in-law had said, 'Your parents are your problem' and refused his request.

Over time, Paula's son and daughter-in-law came to an agreement regarding access to the children. Paula's son had the children for the whole weekend every second weekend, and Paula began to see more of her grandchildren. However, it worried Paula that she never knew when her son and his wife were going to have their next fight. Even though they were separated, they were both impulsive people and Paula felt she had to constantly tread on eggshells and be careful not to say the wrong thing. It was always in the back of her mind, 'At the moment, I am needed. But who knows what's going to happen tomorrow?'

Rather than continue to live with this uncertainty, Paula began to work hard on building up the value of her daughter-in-law in the eyes of the children. She also made an effort to speak with and form a personal relationship with her daughter-in-law that was separate to that of her son. This paid dividends and, over time, despite her broken relationship with Paula's son, her daughter-in-law began to recognise Paula as a caring and decent person whom she could trust and who was good for her children.

By the end of counselling, Paula was of the view that she now had stronger individual relationships with her son, daughter-in-law and grandchildren, even if it was born out of something unpleasant. It was friendlier than it had been for a long time, and the anticipated divorce was not causing as much stress as she previously thought it would. All were agreed that the children were happier because their lives, although different, did not involve as much conflict as when their parents were together.

Collaborative Parenting

Some couples believe that when they separate they will no longer have frequent and intense interaction with their former partner. But if you have children, this is not possible – as parents you remain linked forever, obliged to interact with each other on a regular basis. The challenge for separated couples is to make the ongoing parenting relationship as manageable and as constructive as possible, so that their children receive a balanced, loving upbringing, during which their parents demonstrate collaboration, respect and dignity. (In research carried out with 3,000 couples, it was found that over 70 per cent of couples who sought counselling had children under the age of eleven.)[4]

Popular impressions, media images and stereotypes greatly exaggerate the long-term effects of separation or divorce on children. On average, there are small differences in emotional and social adjustment between children of separated parents and children of intact families. In some instances, especially where there has been a lot of fighting and arguing, separation has a positive effect on children. Children tend to be resilient, adapt well to most changes

---

4. K. McKeown, T. Haase and J. Pratschke, *Distressed Relationships: Does Counselling Help?* (Dublin: Marriage and Relationship Counselling Service, Family Support Agency and Department of Social & Family Affairs, 2004).

in their family roles and life situations and, over time, exhibit normal adjustment. That said, most children and adolescents experience short-term emotional, behavioural and academic difficulties during the separation process. This usually peaks at the point when their parents engage in legal battles. A minority remain vulnerable, particularly in families where there is a high level of antagonism between the separating parents. Following break-ups where there are high levels of conflict and little collaboration, approximately 25 per cent of children experience long-term adjustment problems, compared to roughly 10 per cent of children in first-marriage families.

Collaborative parenting is a key tool in facilitating a smooth transition for parents and children. It is challenging, but ensures that you and your former partner can give your children continued stability and close relationships with both parents and extended families during a time of major change in their lives.

Parenting when the mother and father are together is not easy, and parenting when they are separated demands even more commitment and focus. Putting aside personal issues in order to parent amicably can be extremely difficult and fraught with stress. However, I have found that it is one area where separated couples can agree and, over time, regain some trust in each other – not as husband and wife, but as father and mother.

With the right approach, frame of mind and support, it is possible to initiate and maintain a working parental relationship with your former partner for the sake of your children. You may have separated as husband and wife but you maintain a unique familial and societal bond as mother and father to the same child or children. You have a shared concern and that concern, your children, is the most precious thing in the world to both of you. It is the unconditional love you have for your children that will give you, if tapped into, the power and energy to remain calm, stay consistent and avoid or effectively resolve conflict at this time.

There is also an important self-care aspect to maintaining a good parental relationship: it can be very hard for one adult to provide the amount of time and energy required to parent children. The ferrying of children to various sports and social activities can, in some instances, seem to require a fleet of taxis as opposed to two parents; so imagine how hard that burden would be for one parent.

Joint custody arrangements, especially during and after an acrimonious split, can be draining and exasperating. It can be extremely difficult to get past the painful history you may have with your former partner and overcome any built-up resentment. Making mutual decisions, interacting with each other at drop-off times, or just speaking to a person you'd rather forget all about can seem like impossible tasks. But while it is true that co-parenting isn't an easy solution, it is the best way to ensure your children's needs are met and that children can retain a close relationship with both parents.

The Best Option For Your Children
It may be helpful to start thinking of your relationship with your former partner as a completely new one – one that is entirely about the well-being of your children and not about either of you. Your marriage may be over, but your family is not. Doing what is best for your kids is your priority. The first step to being a responsible parent is to always put your children's needs ahead of your own.

Collaborative parenting ensures your kids recognise and understand that they are more important than the conflict that ended the marriage and relationship. They should be clearly told by both parents that your love for them will prevail despite changing circumstances. This will allow children to:

Feel secure: When confident of the love of both parents, children adjust more quickly and easily to separation and divorce and have better self-esteem.

Benefit from consistency: Collaborative parenting fosters similar rules, discipline and rewards between households, so children know what to expect and what's expected of them.

Better understand problem solving: Children who see their parents continuing to work together are more likely to learn how to effectively and peacefully solve problems.

Have a healthy example to follow: By collaborating and co-operating with the other parent, you are establishing a life pattern your children can carry into the future.

The key to collaborative parenting is to focus on your children. This can be very difficult as it means that your own emotions – any anger, resentment or hurt – must take a back seat to the child's needs. Setting aside such strong feelings may be the hardest part of learning to work collaboratively with your former partner, but it is essential. Staying child-focused can help you if you feel angry or resentful. Keeping a photo of your children on your person can remind you why you need to act with purpose and grace and may help you calm down.

Collaboration recognises your feelings and those of your former spouse, but puts your child's happiness, stability and future well-being before you and your former partner. Vital to this approach is the skill of separating your feelings from your behaviour. It is okay to be hurt and angry, but your feelings do not have to dictate your behaviour. Instead, let what is best for your children motivate your actions.

If You Undermine the Parent, You Undermine the Child

If you saw a stranger or relative telling your child that they were an idiot, untrustworthy and basically a waste of space, what would your response be? Like all good parents you would not accept it. However, a lot of parents forget that a child's well-being is very much based on the child's view of their parents. If the child perceives that their parent is a good, strong, well-liked person, then they, in turn, feel good, strong and happy. If a child perceives that a parent is not liked, respected or loved, then they can also feel that way about themselves. It is crucial that you never vent to or in front of your children about your former partner. Remember that if you do so, you are undermining their parent and therefore undermining your own child.

Children have a tendency to carry the crosses and problems of their parents. Make sure your child is as free as possible from your burdens. You may never completely lose all of your resentment or bitterness about your break-up, but what you can do is compartmentalise those feelings and remind yourself that they are your issues, not your child's. Resolve to keep your issues with your former partner away from your children. Never say negative things about your former partner to your children, or make them feel like they have to choose. Your child has a right to a relationship with his or her other parent that is free of your influence. Friends and therapists can all make good listeners when you need to get negative feelings off your chest. Exercise can also be a healthy outlet for letting off steam. It may seem impossible to stay calm when dealing with a difficult former spouse who has hurt you in the past or has a knack for pushing your buttons. By practicing some of the quick stress relief techniques set out in earlier and later chapters, you can learn to stay in control when the pressure builds.

Communication is Key to Collaboration

Peaceful, consistent and purposeful communication with your former partner is essential to the success of co-parenting – even though it may seem absolutely impossible. It all begins with your mindset. Think about communication with your former partner as having the highest purpose: your child's well-being. Before contact, ask yourself how your language will affect your child and resolve to conduct yourself with dignity. Make your child the focal point of every discussion you have with your former partner.

It is important that you never use children as messengers. When you ask your child to tell the other parent something for you, it puts them in the centre of your conflict. The goal is to keep your child out of your relationship issues, so contact your former partner yourself.

Communication with your former partner is likely to be a tough task. Remember that it is not always necessary to meet in person – speaking over the phone or exchanging texts or emails is fine for the majority of conversations. The goal is to establish conflict-free communication, so see which type of contact works best for you. Whether talking via email, phone or in person, the following methods can help you initiate and maintain effective communication.

Set a business-like tone: Approach the relationship with your former partner as a business partnership, in which the goal is your children's well-being. Speak or write as you would to a colleague – with cordiality, respect and neutrality. Relax and talk slowly.

Make requests: Instead of making statements, which can be misinterpreted as demands, try framing as much as you can as requests. Requests can begin, 'Would you be willing to…?' or 'Can we try…?'

Listen: Communicating with maturity starts with listening. Even if you end up disagreeing, you should at least be able to convey to your former partner that you have understood their point of view. Remember that listening does not signify approval, so you will not lose anything by allowing your former partner to voice their opinions.

Show restraint: Keep in mind that communicating with one another is going to be necessary for the duration of your children's childhood, if not longer. You can train yourself to not overreact to your former partner and, over time, you can become resilient to their capacity to upset you.

Commit to meeting/talking consistently: Frequent communication between parents will convey the message to your children that you are a united front. This may be extremely difficult in the early stages of your separation.

Keep conversations child-focused: You can control the content of your communication. Never let a discussion with your former partner digress into a conversation about your own needs or issues.

Improving the Relationship With Your Former Partner

If you are truly ready to rebuild trust after separation or divorce, be sincere about your efforts. Remember your children's best interests as you move forward to improve your relationship.

Ask their opinion: This fairly simple technique can jump-start positive communications. Choose an issue related to your child that you do not feel especially strongly about and ask for your former partner's input. This demonstrates that you value their opinion when it comes to parenting.

Apologise: When you are sorry about something, take the time to apologise sincerely – even if the incident happened a long time ago. Apologising can be very powerful in moving your relationship away from being adversaries.

Latitude: If your child's special outing with your former partner is going to cut into your time with your child by a short amount, graciously let it be. Remember that it is all about what is best for your child. Plus, when you show flexibility, your former partner is more likely to be flexible with you.

Parenting is full of decisions you'll have to make with your former partner, whether you like each another or not. Cooperating and communicating without blow-ups or bickering makes decision-making far easier on everybody. If you aim for consistency and geniality, the details of child-rearing decisions tend to fall into place.

Consistency is Key

It is healthy for children to be exposed to different perspectives and to learn to be flexible, but they also need to know they are living under the same basic set of expectations in each home. Aiming for consistency between your home and that of your former partner avoids confusion for your children.

Rules don't have to be exactly the same between two households, but if you and your former spouse establish generally consistent guidelines, your children will not have to bounce back and forth between two radically different disciplinary environments. Important lifestyle rules, like homework issues, bedtimes and off-limit activities, should be followed in both households.

Discipline means trying to follow similar systems of consequences for broken rules, even if the infraction didn't happen under your roof. So, if the children have lost privileges while at one parent's house, then follow-through with the restriction must happen when they go to the other parent's house. The same can be done for rewarding good behaviour.

Schedules should aim for some consistency in your child's routine. Making meals, homework and bedtimes similar in both houses can go a long way toward your child's adjustment to having two homes.

Critical Life Issues

Major decisions need to be made by both you and your former partner about issues that will affect your children's future. Being open, honest and straightforward about important issues is crucial to your children's well-being.

Medical needs: Effective co-parenting can help parents focus on the best medical care for the child and can reduce anxiety for everyone. Whether you decide to designate one parent to communicate primarily with healthcare professionals or attend medical appointments together, keep one another in the loop.

Education: School plays a major role in providing a stable environment for your children, so be sure to let them know about changes to your child's living situation. Speak with your former partner ahead of time about class timetables, extra-curricular activities and parent–teacher meetings, and be polite to him or her at any school or sports events you both attend.

Financial issues: The cost of maintaining two separate households can strain your attempts to be effective parents. Set a realistic budget and keep accurate records for shared expenses. Be gracious if your former partner provides opportunities for your children that you cannot provide.

Disagreements

Like all parents, separated couples are bound to disagree over certain issues. Keep the following in mind as you try to come to consensus with your former partner.

Respect can go a long way: Simple manners are often neglected between parents, even though they should be the foundation for collaborative parenting. Being considerate and respectful includes letting your former partner know about school events, being flexible about your schedule when possible and taking their opinion seriously.

Keep talking: It might sound tedious, but if you disagree about something important, you will need to continue to communicate about the topic. Never discuss your differences of opinions with or in front of your child. If you still can't agree, you may need to talk to a third party, like a therapist or mediator.

Don't sweat the small stuff: If you disagree about important issues like a medical procedure or choice of school for your child, by all means keep the discussion going. But if you want your child in bed by 7.30 p.m. and your former partner says 8.00 p.m., try to let it go and save your energy for the bigger issues.

Compromise: You will need to come around to your former spouse's point of view as often as he or she will need to come around to yours. It may not always be your first choice, but compromise allows you both to 'win' and makes you more likely to be flexible in the future.

Living in Two Houses

The actual move from one household to another, whether it happens every few days, every weekend or more infrequently, can be very hard for children. Transitions like this represent a major change in your children's reality. Every reunion with one parent is also a separation with the other; every 'hello' is also a 'goodbye'. In joint custody arrangements, transition time is inevitable, but there are many things you can do to help make exchanges and transitions easier, both when your children leave and return to your home.

You can use the following strategies to help make transitions easier:

Help children anticipate change: Remind children they will be leaving for the other parent's house a day or two before the visit.

Pack in advance: Depending on their age, help children pack their bags well before they leave so that they don't forget anything they might miss. Encourage packing familiar reminders, like a special stuffed toy or photograph.

Double up: To make packing simpler and make children feel more comfortable when staying with both parents, keep certain basics – toothbrush, hairbrush, pyjamas – at both houses.

Stay positive: It is hard for any parent to be parted from their children, but it is important that you stay positive as they prepare to leave your house.

Always drop off, never pick up the child: It is a good idea to avoid collecting your child from the other parent, so that you don't risk interrupting or curtailing a special moment. Drop off your child at the other parent's house instead. Always drop them off on time.

Keep things low-key when the child returns: When children first re-enter your home, try to have some down-time together – read a book or do some other quiet activity.

Allow the child space: Children often need a little time to adjust to the transition. If they seem to need some space, leave them be and do something else nearby. In time, things will get back to normal.

Establish a special routine: Play a game or serve the same special meal each time your child returns. Children thrive on routine – if they know exactly what to expect when they return to you, it can help the transition.

When Kids say 'No'

Sometimes children refuse to leave one parent to be with the other. Although this can be a difficult situation, it is also common for children in joint custody.

Find the cause: The problem may be one that is easy to resolve, like paying more attention to your child, making a change in discipline style or having more toys or other entertainment. Or it may be that an emotional reason is at hand, such as conflict or misunderstanding. Talk to your child about their refusal.

Go with the flow: Whether you have detected the reason for the refusal or not, try to give your child the space and time that they obviously need. It may have nothing to do with you at all. And take heart: most cases of visitation refusal are temporary.

Talk to your former partner: A discussion with your former partner about the refusal may be challenging and emotional, but can help you to figure out what the problem is. Try to be sensitive and understanding as you discuss this touchy subject.

Dealing With Holidays and Special Occasions

In families where parents are separated, things are a little harder for children during school holidays and special occasions. They may need a little extra love and support.

They will sometimes reflect back on past holidays before the relationship broke down. The challenges of their new situation can cause children to feel extremely overwhelmed at these times.

To help your children stay balanced and to give them a positive experience, do not put them on the spot by asking questions like, 'Who do you want to spend Christmas or New Year with?' Children love and are loyal to both parents and should not feel torn between them. Once plans are agreed, let your children know their holiday visitation plans well ahead of time. Last-minute planning can cause stress. Do not be afraid of starting new traditions if the old ones conflict with the children seeing both parents or are too difficult for a single parent to carry out. Both parents should get together and decide on how the children's time will be spent, taking into consideration what the children would prefer.

Both parents should work together to simplify their respective family obligations. Children who are over-scheduled can feel like they are being pulled in different directions. This will increase the stress on both the parents and children. Follow through on the commitments you have made to your children. Disappointment during the holidays can make it stressful for everyone. So make sure to do what you have promised.

At Christmas and on birthdays, more than any other time of the year, put your children's needs above your own. You may disagree with your former spouse on many topics, but unless it is something that may harm the child, do the best to get along with them. Parents need to be careful not to compete with each other over who gives the best gift. Show your love through words and by spending time with your child. Remember that they will benefit more from your presence than from presents. Plan visits with both sides of the extended family. Keep in mind that grandparents, cousins, aunts and uncles are a very special part of the holidays.

Parenting Plans

A parenting plan acts as the framework within which you will interact together for as long as your child is a minor, so getting it right the first time is critical to everyone's well-being. Many parents feel overwhelmed at the prospect of creating their parenting plan agreement because there is so much information to consider. Fortunately, computer software has been developed for the purpose of creating custody agreements and plans quickly and easily.

Most counsellors and mediators provide an opportunity to put together such a plan, including a child visitation schedule and agreement. Getting a parenting plan completed as early as possible will save you much time and money.

Child custody and co-parenting a child, and how you spend your parenting time with that child, will have a profound effect on your child's development and will influence how they see the world as an adult. Make certain you demonstrate to your child that being reasonable, consistent and courteous are core values. Most children emulate what you do more than what you say, so ensure your behaviour sets a good example. Getting age-appropriate children involved in the planning can help provide certainty and stability.

The key elements to a solid parenting plan are:

Residential schedule: This schedule repeats itself from month to month, detailing what times the child spends at home and when the child is with the non-custodial parent, the transportation involved and the times for arrival and departure.

Holiday schedule: A semi-fixed schedule detailing the year's holidays and where and with whom the child will spend their time.

Activities and events: If it is a repeat event, such as sports, music lessons and the like, the mother may take the child to the event one month and the father the next month. Alternatively, a parent may concentrate on certain activities, e.g. the father may take the child to hockey, while the mother takes them to drama club. Other events might include friends' birthday parties, concerts, group trips and so on. It is important to have a schedule covering which parent will be there for supervision and transportation to and from all events and activities.

When co-parenting, too many parents get into the way of thinking that the scheduling framework is for their convenience and lose sight of its intended purpose: the child's well-being. Parenting plans function best when each parent is respectful and considerate of the other's time and effort. The opposite can also be true: some parents deliberately interfere with a visitation schedule as a way to irritate their former partner, not realising that the rancour probably does more damage to the child than it does to the other parent.

If you are successful in developing and agreeing your parenting plan before it is asked of you from the court, you will be well on your way to a more peaceful, balanced life for your child, for yourself and for your former partner.

Collaborative parenting is a key component of moving on when love breaks down, while ensuring that your children continue to enjoy the love of both parents. With the right tools and frame of mind it is possible to initiate and maintain a cordial working relationship with your former partner for the sake of your children. It is the unconditional love you have for your children that will give you the power and energy to remain calm, stay consistent and avoid or effectively resolve conflict with your former partner.

Below are some final things to keep in mind for collaborative parenting during and after a difficult break-up. Each situation is different so all of these may not apply in your case, but try to remember as many as possible. Your children will thank you for it.

For All Separated or Divorced Parents:
- Your children are hurting as much or more than you are.
- Don't try to get them to take sides.
- Your children still need two parents involved in their lives.
- Try to make major parenting decisions together.
- Be flexible with visitation schedules when possible.
- Give your children as much say as possible on when they see their other parent.
- Your children will likely still have hopes of you reuniting with your former partner for years after the relationship ends.
- Your children may not be supportive of you dating.
- Your children don't want to hear you undermining their other parent.

- Your children don't want to be used as messengers.
- Don't over-extend yourself financially to maintain all of their pre-separation activities and lifestyle.

For Custodial Parents:
- Your children still love and miss the non-custodial parent.
- Keep the non-custodial parent informed of school, sports and social events.
- Don't use the excuse that the child support was late for not doing things, even if that is the reason.

For Non-Custodial Parents:
- Your children want to know you care. Do this by spending time with them.
- Your children are hurt deeply if you don't show up when you are supposed to.
- Don't substitute money or gifts for spending time with your children.
- Your children want you to come to their school, sports or social events.
- Your children want to hear from you regularly, even if you can't be with them.
- You have a moral and legal obligation to pay child support. Do it.
- Don't expect all of your support money to be spent specifically on the kids. That's not how it works.

Mary and Michael

Mary and Michael had been married for sixteen years. Mary worked part-time in a crèche, while Michael was the main earner, working in the information technology sector. They had two children: a boy, aged thirteen, and a girl, aged fifteen. Michael had worked long hours in the past and left most of the parenting to Mary, but as the children grew older, Michael was showing more interest in spending time with them.

Mary and Michael had been separated for two years when we first met. Michael was still very upset with the separation and wanted to reconcile. However, the pressing issue was his lack of contact with the children. Mary said that Michael was frequently upset when he came over to pick up the children. In fact, he often cried and begged Mary to take him back. He did this in the presence of the children, which upset them too. Mary said the children did not want to go on visits with their father as they were closer to her and did not like seeing their father so visibly shaken.

We had a few individual sessions and then both Michael and Mary attended counselling together. We discussed Michael's emotional state. We also agreed that there was no possibility of reconciliation, but that Michael needed help coming to terms with the separation. Mary gained an understanding of Michael's position, particularly his worries and anxieties about being a good father. They both learned a lot about the dynamics of their new relationship and how to approach each other in a more sensitive way.

After four sessions, Mary and Michael reviewed and signed a participation agreement, dealing with some urgent issues related to the payment of bills. They also discussed retaining my help as a counsellor to help them work through their parenting issues. As a result, the process started positively.

I also met with the children several times and subsequently met with Mary and Michael together to share my insights and thoughts about the children. We worked through several pressing parenting issues, such as attendance at extra-curricular activities, the introduction of new partners (Mary had started dating) and how to communicate regarding the children.

We then met to work out when the children would be in Michael's care. The counselling (and perhaps also the passage of time) had really helped Michael to accept Mary's decision to separate and that, in time, a divorce would occur. Consequently, he was more emotionally stable around the children and their relationship was improving.

The parties reached an agreement for the children to see their father every Sunday afternoon for the first couple of weeks, the whole day for the next couple of weeks and then, finally, for a full day and overnight. The children were happy with the new arrangement and the gradual increase over time also gave Mary a chance to adjust to being apart from them.

After three months, we had a family meeting. We discussed each person's experience of the custody arrangement so far. Following this, the parents were able to agree on a time-sharing regime for the children that met their needs. We drafted an agreement that was signed by both parties. Mary and Michael knew that the agreement they signed that day might have to be adjusted as the needs of the children and the circumstances of their own lives changed, but they felt they had developed a good plan that worked for now. The children were adjusting well to their new circumstances. Mary and Michael were starting to develop a new relationship based solely on working together as parents. They were moving in the right direction. It was an excellent resolution for everyone, especially the children, whose voices and needs were respected and met.

Creating a Safe Space for Children

Opinions differ on the effect relationship breakdown has on children. Some experts state that children of divorced couples have trouble adapting in later life because of their experience with broken or faulty attachment bonds. These children are said to have no accurate template for successful relationships to replicate in their adult lives. Others suggest that children of divorced parents adapt to life's situations and relationships within normal ranges when compared to their peers because they have learned early to adapt to situations and realise that life is not always perfect. However, what all agree upon is that there is an undeniable bond between children and their parents and that marriage constitutes a highly significant form of attachment bond that has consequences when broken.

No matter how much a husband and wife grow to dislike each other, most separating parents ask themselves some tough questions about what their actions will do to their children. They wonder about how the children will make sense of what is happening. How will they react to both parents as the family changes? Will they adjust well? Will their performance in school suffer? Will they withdraw from their friends, and perhaps suffer some permanent emotional harm? Perhaps the bottom line for most parents is whether or not their children will come through the break-up and emerge as reasonably healthy adults. Certainly most children do, and many are better off than if they had remained in a family of arguing and unhappy members.

This chapter sets out some of the knowledge learned from research in this area and from over twenty years of personal practice. However, as you read, bear in mind that each child is unique, and not all children experience the difficulties defined and explored below. This chapter is an overview of the most common problems experienced by children during a relationship breakdown. To help the reader focus in on their child's possible perspective, the key issues are addressed with relevance to children of different age groups.

Infants and Preschool-Age Children

For preschool-age children, the most common reactions to their parents separating are fear, confusion and guilt. Young children lack the ability to understand what is happening and why. Their primitive logic can lead them to assume that if Dad can leave their daily life, Mum can too (or vice versa), and that if Mum and Dad can stop loving each other, they can also stop loving the children. They often worry about who will take care of them, whether there will be enough food, enough money, a house to live in, and so forth.

Parents of children this age will often observe a tendency to revert to earlier forms of behaviour, such as reclaiming a security blanket, problems in toileting, emotional clinging, disobedience, night terrors and fear of separating from their parents even for short periods. There may be strange fantasies about what has happened to cause the absence of a parent, disruptions in play activities and an increase in aggression. It is common for young children to believe that they are responsible for the break-up of the family, and that if they had only been better behaved, Dad or Mum would have stayed. If they see their parent being very upset, bright pre-schoolers and older children may hide their own distress so as not to be an additional burden.

What to do:
Young children need clear and frequent reassurances that they will be taken care of, that both Mum and Dad still love them, that they are still a family even though they will have different living arrangements. They need simple explanations about why the separation is occurring to reassure them that the problems are between Mum and Dad, and that the break-up is not their fault. They also need an opportunity to express their fears and concerns. Parents should frequently set aside time to talk to their preschool-aged children about their feelings.

Children need to spend meaningful one-to-one time with each parent, as frequently as possible. A two-week period of absence from a parent is too painful for young children, most of whom are intensely dissatisfied with the standard visitation schedule of every other weekend. For children under three years old, one-week absences are too long, as their sense of time is very different from that of older children. For infants, daily contact with both parents is the preferred option.

Young School-Age Children
The most typical response of children in this age group (5–8 years) is grief, usually expressed through crying (especially among boys), and a deep yearning for the departed parent,

usually the father. Research shows that the children will miss the absent parent acutely, regardless of the quality of their relationship before the break-up. Anger toward the absent parent will not usually be expressed, while considerable anger may be directed toward the remaining parent. When visitation is greatly reduced, the children usually believe that the parent who has moved out has stopped loving them.

One of the most serious and common burdens experienced by children at this age is the emotional tug-of-war that occurs when one or both parents try to get the child to side with them. Parents may unintentionally force the child into listening to their negative view of the other parent. In this situation the worst effected are the children, who are caught in the middle.

At this age, children hope and believe that someday Mum and Dad will get back together, and will feel a strong sense of responsibility to take care of their parents, despite their own emotional needs. Early signs that your child is looking and acting fine do not guarantee the absence of emotional problems much later on.

What to do:
Children of all ages, but especially children in this age group, need to be protected from the parents' disappointments and anger. Children should not be pressured to take sides. Avoid criticising and undermining the other parent in front of the children at all costs. What they need most at this time is the reassurance from both parents that although Mum and Dad don't get along well enough to continue living together, they both still love and will take care of the children. It is also critical that the children be assured that even though one parent has moved to a new home, they

will still be able to be with that parent, and that it is okay to still love that parent.

Older School-Age Children

This older age group (9–12 years) typically differs from the younger age group in their reaction to the relationship breakdown, largely because of their more advanced level of intellectual development. They now have at least a basic ability to see the various points of view in a situation. Most of these children are able to understand some of the reasons for the relationship breakdown and will bravely try to make the best of it.

However, these children will often cover up the distress that they are feeling (for example, saying that they see their father enough, or that they don't feel rejected, when in fact they miss him terribly). In part, these denials may be a result of their sensitivity to the custodial parent's expressed anger toward the other parent. A significant minority of children at this age (about a quarter) will become an ally of one parent (usually the mother) in the parental battle. While they are better able than their younger siblings to see both sides in a dispute, they nonetheless tend to see things in rather black-and-white terms. This results in a need to label one parent as the good guy and one as the villain.

Children at this age may also try to undo the separation or divorce, perhaps to counteract their own sense of powerlessness in the situation. They are likely to experience intense anger, of which they are fully aware, unlike their younger siblings. Part of this anger is a natural outcome of the break-up of the family. It is also partly because they often see a double standard in their parents' behaviour. There may be visible inconsistency between the parents' discipline of the child and (at least in the child's eyes) their own inappropriate actions.

Also common at this age are a seriously shaken identity and a variety of physical complaints – including infections, headaches, stomach aches, asthma, etc. – aggravated by the stress the child is experiencing. Many paediatricians report that these physical symptoms bring children of separated parents to their offices far more often than children in intact families. It is important to let your family doctor and the children's teachers know about the changes in the family. They can best assist your child's adjustment if they have at least a basic understanding of the sources of stress.

What to do:
It is important for both parents to have extensive conversations with children of this age about the break-up and its aftermath, in order to make it easier for children to voice their feelings. The children are quite capable of expressing their concerns and fears, and will have at least a simple understanding of the parents' points of view. It is appropriate to let them know that Mum and Dad disagree about their own personal lives, but that there is still much agreement about the children's lives. Parents should then work very hard to make that agreement happen.

The child's anger needs to be acknowledged. And both parents need to try to change those things that the children find most upsetting. Often, what the children are most upset about is the breakdown itself, and they will yearn for reconciliation. If this is unrealistic (and it usually is), this should be expressed clearly to the children.

Again, as with younger children, the parents' anger toward each other must be hidden from the children by minimising any conflict in their presence and by frequently showing the children that they have permission to love the other parent. This can be done by encouraging the children to call or write letters, and by helping them to buy birthday, Christmas and Mother's or Father's Day cards and gifts for the other parent. It is also helpful to occasionally say positive things about the other parent in front of the children.

It is critical to avoid pressure for the children to choose sides. This is destructive to their relationship with the other parent and inevitably leads to more stress and even to resentment toward both parents.

Adolescents

Children in the 13–18 age group have certain advantages over younger children because they are more developed, both socially and intellectually, and therefore have more resources to deal with the family break-up. Furthermore, their primary orientation during this period is their peer group rather than the family (although keep in mind that this can also mean that many of the problems they will encounter may be hidden from parents).

Among the more common and enduring problems is the loss of the parent–child relationship, which is a major source of support during adolescence. The absence of two involved parents during this period of development lessens the guidance that adolescents require. For many, the lack of consistency in discipline is unsettling. It is not unusual for teenagers to act out their anger and frustration by gravitating toward deviant peers and engaging in substance abuse and sexual promiscuity.

Many teenagers find it necessary to 'compact' their period of growing up by assuming greater responsibilities in the family. About a third become more involved in family life, but another third become removed. While some teenagers respond with maturity and moral growth (vowing to do better than their parents), many will have lasting concerns about their own intimate relationships, worrying about sex and marriage well into adulthood. They are likely to marry earlier, however, and to have higher than normal divorce rates. In part this is due to hasty decisions to marry, combined with a poor choice of partner.

What to do:
Adolescents will usually be able to tolerate the ambiguities involved in a break-up and realise that there are two sides to the story. They should be encouraged to ask questions and should be given clear and honest replies. Parents will be most helpful if they can state their own views and then try to state objectively and fairly the other parent's views. The latter may be very hard for most parents to do. As an alternative, they should encourage their children to ask questions and voice their own concerns about the other parent. In doing so, the adolescent will feel less pressure to choose sides, and begin to appreciate that while each parent may see the situation differently, there may be truth to both sides. Most importantly, the parents' honesty will help to re-establish trust. Teenagers are better able to detect dishonesty, manipulation and double standards than younger children, so parents who are dishonest run the risk of losing their teenagers' respect.

Parents need to learn good communication skills, such as actively listening to their children and giving blame-free messages about their own feelings and reactions. These are often called 'I messages'. For example, if a child is upset and criticises you, you might say, 'I feel hurt when you say those things', as opposed to, 'You're being a mouthy brat. You sound just like your mother/father.'

Teenagers often assume greater family responsibilities in the event of a break-up, especially if there are younger children in the family. However, in spite of the temptation to do so, parents must avoid relying upon their older children as a source of emotional support. While some will do a good job of helping out a depressed and insecure parent, this can be an overwhelming emotional burden, even for a reasonably mature teenager. Separating parents do need emotional support, but they should foster close friendships with other adults and/or seek out help from a mental health professional. Making children feel responsible for parental well-being and happiness can be a crippling experience during a time when they are trying to decipher their own emotions and busy exploring their own relationships.

Telling the Children

Ideally, both mother and father should deliver news of the break-up together, no matter how uncomfortable the prospect makes them. Adolescents and even pre-teens usually understand what it means when adults separate, so it's best to give it to them straight, minus inappropriate details. Chances are they are more aware of the problems in the marriage than most parents imagine.

One crucial point to convey is that although the two adults are separating as husband and wife, they will never stop being their parents. Try saying something like, 'We both love you very, very much and always will. That will never change.' Another crucial point is to reassure them that this is strictly between the two of you and that they are in no way responsible for your decision. You will be eliminating this seed of anxiety without them having to ask.

Tell them, as lovingly as possible, that they will now have two homes, e.g. 'We haven't worked out all the details, but most of the time you'll live with your mother right here. Same house, same school. As soon as I get settled, you'll live with me the rest of the time, like on weekends and holidays.' It is important that you say 'live with' and not 'visit'. Volunteer as much information as you can about living arrangements to ease their fears. If possible, allow at least a few weeks between the announcement and the day a parent moves out of the home.

The conversation will continue to unfold over the next few days, weeks and months. Expect tears, protestations and a barrage of questions. Top of the list is often, 'Why are you splitting up? Didn't you used to love each other?' Emphasise the good aspects of your life together but explain that sometimes people who were once very much in love can grow apart. Tell them that feelings can change over the years and, as much as you have tried to restore your marriage to the way it used to be, you have both come to the sad conclusion that the relationship is beyond repair and that a separation is best for everyone.

In moments of anger and hurt, a child may blame one parent – often the residential parent – for the split: 'You could have tried harder to work things out!' or 'Why did you make Dad leave?' While this type of comment appears unfair, try not to take the accusation to heart or become defensive. In response, you might say: 'I understand that you're sad. We are, too. You may feel that I am more at fault than your father, but you don't know the full story. There are other ways of looking at what happened. When you're not so angry, let's talk more about it.'

When a child asks if there is a chance of reconciliation, it is important not to encourage this possibility. Like the identical twin sisters in *The Parent Trap*, adolescents need little encouragement to dream about reuniting their estranged parents. One tactic, more common among girls, is to behave like the perfect child. The reverse strategy is to get into so much trouble that a concerned mum and dad forget their differences and come to the rescue. Either reaction is a form of denial, an attempt to avoid facing the painful reality of what has happened to the family, and may require professional guidance.

The Effect on School

There is considerable research to show that children dealing with their parents' relationship breakdown can have a difficult time at school too. Pre-schoolers often enter school at a particular disadvantage, not being as ready as other children either socially or intellectually. Older children often have difficulty paying attention, so grades usually suffer. And some children, especially boys, may have behavioural problems.

Parents should speak to teachers and guidance counsellors as soon as possible about a family disruption or break-up that has occurred or is about to occur. This will enable the teacher to understand many of the child's problems and to provide support during a period of adjustment. Parent–teacher communication should occur regularly to foster a coordinated, supportive approach that will help the child master academic and social tasks at school.

Parents should request that their children be included in a support group at school, or suggest that one be started, as these are very helpful. Parents should show even greater interest than usual in their children's school activities and encourage frequent discussion of any problems that occur at school.

Avoid Alienating Your Children

The immediate distress for children surrounding parental separation fades with time, and the great majority of children go on to function as healthy adults. However, for some, it is an emotionally stressful and complex transition and continues to affect them into adulthood.

My own experience working with children and adults points to the absolute need to avoid alienating children during a relationship breakdown. The best way to do this is to give them space and time, but most of all, not to involve them in parental fighting. Adults can sometimes fall into the blame game and it typically results in children who fell alienated, who are consumed with hatred for one or both parents – usually for one, targeted parent. They deny any positive past experiences and reject all contact and communication. Once loved and valued parents can, seemingly overnight, become hated and feared. One parent is perceived as perfect, while the other is perceived as wholly flawed.

This is in contrast to the fact that most children have mixed feelings about even the best of parents and can usually talk about each as having both good and bad qualities. Even though alienated children appear to be unduly influenced by one parent's negativity, they will adamantly insist that the decision to reject the targeted parent is theirs alone.

Alienated children typically appear rude, ungrateful, spiteful and cold towards the targeted parent, and they appear to be impervious to feelings of guilt over their harsh treatment. Gratitude for gifts, favours or support provided by the targeted parent can be non-existent. Alienated children will often try to get whatever they can from that parent, declaring that it is owed to them.

Helping Men Cope

It is accepted that all individuals are capable of responding to situations beyond gender sterotypes. However, while men and women are the same species, their perceptions, experiences and reactions to life's challenges can be very different. This may be attributable to their biological differences but also to subconsciously entrenched cultural gender paradigms, which teach people how to think and behave as men and women. The next two chapters aim to help both men and women involved in a relationship break-up to adjust to their situation, but also to give each person an understanding of what their former partner might be thinking and the challenges they may be facing. The ultimate goal is a separation that leaves both individuals with their dignity intact, while offering hope for the future.

The end of a marriage or long-term relationship is one of the most traumatic things that can happen to a man. The majority of separated men I have worked with refer at some stage to being hit with the reality that they have lost their wife, kids, house, money, self-esteem and self-respect. Doctor Ron Levant, a professor at Harvard University, coined the term 'normative male' to illustrate his finding that men can suffer from the conditioning of our modern culture, which causes them to be underdeveloped emotionally. Men have developed two primary responses to emotional issues: vulnerable feelings – including fear, hurt and shame – are dealt with through anger, the 'manly' response; nurturing feelings – including caring, warmth, connectedness and intimacy –are channelled by men through physicality and activity.

Most men function through action empathy as opposed to emotional empathy. Action empathy is the attempt to enter into another person's point of view, knowing (or thinking that one knows) what the other person is likely to do. That is why men are keen to want to fix situations, as fixing is a 'doing' activity. It is not good for most men to be in a position where they feel they lack control.

A major problem for some men is a lack of awareness of their emotions, particularly negative ones. Emotions originate in the limbic system within the brain, before moving to the autonomic and endocrine systems, which engage the muscles and skeletal systems, which in turn engage the flight or fight activities (doing). The cognitive awareness of the emotion is the last thing to be experienced. Many men stop the emotional process at the third step, thus cutting off the cognitive awareness of the emotional experience. For some reason, men tend to control their emotions at this point. The result of stopping the emotional process at step three is that emotions may become somatised in the body. This is manifested in physical symptoms such as constrictions to the chest, throat or face; shortness of breath; upset stomach; headache; backache; tension in the shoulders; insomnia; high blood pressure; and heart disease. Separation or divorce can end in trips to the doctor due to high stress levels and a decline in physical well-being.

This lack of emotional processing often means that men do not appreciate the gravity of the situation, and many unintentionally ignore the issues and problems until it is too late. Even when the relationship has ended, men tend to deny the reality and believe that when their partner 'calms down' things will return to normal. This type of thinking only prolongs the agony. The earlier a man can face the reality of the situation and accept that the marriage is over, the quicker he can begin the task of finding happiness.

The matter is further exacerbated by the fact that marriage boosts the mental and physical health of men, although most do not appreciate this fact. Being in a long-term, committed relationship improves men's diet, self-image and mental health, and reduces the chance of premature death by 15 per cent. The networks of supportive relationships, beginning with the spouse and extending out into the community, assists men in leading healthier lifestyles than their single counterparts. Put simply, married men are more likely to eat healthily, have more friends and take better care of themselves. However, when love breaks down, so can the psychological and social networks that encourage and facilitate men in caring for themselves.

Working closely with men for over twenty years, I have found that there is no greater emotional pain that can be inflicted than his wife's announcement that she wants a separation or divorce. Even if both parties have been aware of problems in the relationship for some time (and one would assume that the announcement comes as no great surprise), the actual declaration can be similar to acute physical trauma for many men. The relationship has ended, and the man feels rejected. Such a blow to a man's emotional equilibrium is just about the most damaging thing they will have to face in their lifetime, second only to the death of a child or a loved one. A major problem is that many men will not take time to recognise and accept their thoughts and emotions. Rather, they concentrate on money – spousal maintenance, child support and loss of assets – because it is easier to address tangible things rather than recognise and speak about underlying emotions.

In the majority of cases, it is the woman who will have initiated the separation. This can lead to a more extreme grief reaction in the male partner. They may feel the emotions expressed in the chapter on grief and loss in a more profound way, leading to decreased self-esteem, insecurity, anger, a desire to 'get even' or a fantasy to reconcile. While all of these feelings are common, men should remember that it takes two to end a relationship. It is important to avoid falling into the trap of blaming everything on their former wife, which can sometimes lead to acting out these feelings of anger.

While both men and women have a high risk of depression after a family break-up, most studies reveal that the male risk is higher. One Canadian study followed couples after the dissolution of their marriages. Separated or divorced men aged forty to sixty-four were six times more likely to report an episode of depression than men who remained married. The study, even after controlling for other variables such as income, social support, the presence of children and a history of depression, found that divorced men were still three times more likely to be depressed than married men.

At some point, men begin to see through the fog of emotion. Male clients often speak of lying awake in bed at night, reviewing the details of their marriage – thinking that in this or that circumstance, they could have been a better husband. As a result, they often beg for another chance. These thoughts are only natural, but they cannot put a marriage back together, and any attempts to try one more time at this late stage only causes greater pain. Rather, the man must accept that their marriage is over and busy their mind and themselves with activities to ensure a happy future.

Children

Following a break-up, men are more likely to lose custody of their children and to experience a marked change in parental responsibility. Marriage breakdown is hard on everyone. Women and children also take a big financial hit, lose their friends, and go through many of the same things that men do. However, if there are younger children in the family, women will continue to have the company of their kids, while, more often than not, the father can be left all alone for long periods. It is essential to remember that while you are not a husband, you are most definitely still a father.

There are a lot of ways in which fathers can continue to play an active role. The most critical is to stay in touch – in person, by phone, by email, or by regular mail. Make the time you spend with your children meaningful.

By remaining emotionally and physically available to your children you will help both them and yourself. Men must allow themselves to be aware of their feelings so they can empathise with their children. Then they must take whatever steps necessary to make themselves available to their children. Children whose fathers are involved in their lives do better in school and are less likely to become teen parents or turn to drugs, alcohol or crime. Children with involved fathers also tend to manage their emotions better and are less likely to resort to violence.

Break-ups involving children are often complicated, but the more responsibility you can take in your children's lives, the happier your child's mother will be. When both parents are happy, it makes for a better, albeit different, parental relationship and, consequently, better parents. Building a new relationship with your former partner and maintaining your network are essential to enable your child to thrive during and after your break-up.

It is imperative to show respect for your former partner. Being an involved father means recognising all the ways in which your partner keeps the family running and respecting the decisions she makes when you are unavailable. It is also imperative to be aware of the need to communicate. If you don't like the status quo, let your former partner know. If she seems reluctant at first to share the role of child nurturer with you, do not take it too personally. Give her time to recognise that you are serious about wanting to participate more and that you are competent and sincerely motivated to be an engaged parent.

Dealing with Anger

Some men have the propensity to become angry with their former partner and the world in general. If I was to pick one aspect of relationship breakdown that derails a man's ability to cope and recover, it is this toxic anger. In the whirlpool of shock and grief that separating couples go through, anger tends to be the most dominant emotion in men. All emotions are good and it is important to get anger out of your system. However, if we ignore certain emotions or allow them to grow out of control, they become toxic and can hurt us both psychologically and physically. I am not talking about the brief moments of rage and self-pity that you eventually move out of once the initial shock wears off and you adjust, I am talking about the long-term anger, resentment and bitterness that can follow a person through their life. A helpful way to resolve this feeling is to understand that anger and sadness are different sides of the same coin. Instead of acting out the anger, spend some time looking for and appreciating the sadness underneath.

If you are going through a separation or divorce you will know this anger well: the sense of being so wronged that you want to lash out. You want someone to notice, someone to feel your wrath and be humbled, apologise or something similar. It is an instinctual reaction to make ourselves feel more powerful, to try to obtain some sort of supplication from another by righteous rage that stems from an injustice or hurt.

In ancient societies, strength and power determined justice and law. However, anger these days does not achieve a huge amount. When has shouting at someone ever really produced a good long-term result? When has being angry ever changed a situation for the better? Anger is just a triggered defensive reaction to a perceived injustice. People often fly off the handle even when they are clearly in the wrong; it all comes down to perception.

It is important to understand that anger can fester to become bitterness and resentment. You cannot maintain a raging anger, but many people manage to maintain a simmering loathing of their former wife, themselves, lawyers etc. This is more dangerous than the initial rage, which can often fade quickly. Holding on to a grudge can be a hindrance to your mental health for years to come and will hurt your existing and future relationships and outlook on life.

It is necessary to recognise, accept and work through this strong emotion. Anger is the process of projecting your own sense of hurt and frustration onto another person. It is such a volatile and all-consuming emotion that unless you give it an outlet, it will eat you alive. The thing to do is to understand your anger and manage it in a manner that will benefit you. Regardless of how you do it, it is an absolute necessity that you let it all out. The sooner you get rid of it, the sooner you will be able to get on with your life, regain your mental health and position yourself for happiness. There will come a day when you will no longer be bothered by thoughts of your former partner. It won't even bother you when you see them with another person, and that will be the day when you have finally accepted that your marriage is over. You will have truly let go and will be ready for a new life.

Forgiveness

The key to coping and recovery for men and to letting go of the anger is forgiveness. The act of forgiveness gives you a grace that can have lasting positive consequences in your life. Yet forgiveness has many pre-conceptions attached to it that can stop people from embracing it.

Forgiveness is not about forgetting problems, actions or insults that have occurred. Whatever happened has happened, and must serve as a reminder. Neither is it about excusing the actions of your former partner or yourself or giving permission for these behaviours to continue.

It is also important to note that forgiveness is not necessarily linked with reconciliation. Just because you forgive someone does not mean you need to enter into a relationship again. That is a separate issue. Just remember, you are trying to make a new life, not rebuild the old one.

Forgiveness is a release from anger. It is a way to acknowledge hurt and to set it free, instead of keeping it in your heart. It is a letting go of the need for vengeance, so that you can mentally untie yourself from the negative emotions of the break-up and live your life without burden. To free yourself of anger you must forgive those who have wronged you, because anger will never make anything better in your life. You must let it go and move on, because emotionally it is crippling, and logically it achieves nothing.

Finally, boredom and loneliness is a problem for many men following relationship breakdown. Men who successfully overcome boredom and loneliness in their life usually recognise that both of these problems are self-induced. That is, if you are bored or lonely, it is because you are allowing yourself to be. Boredom is generally a form of emotional anaesthesia, brought about by the person who is bored because he does not want to experience his own feelings. It is a form of mental numbness that keeps people from changing and growing. The solution is quite simple: get involved in something rather than allowing yourself to sit and do nothing. Past clients have opted to socialise with neighbours and old friends; others have joined local sports teams and social clubs. What these varied activities have in common is that they involve getting out and meeting others.

Loneliness is basically a different form of boredom. A person feels lonely when they cannot think of anything they want to do; thus, they begin feeling sorry for themselves, thinking no one cares about them. In order not to be lonely, you have to start thinking of things you might enjoy doing and then invite other people to join you in doing those things. It can be as simple as that. To be happy, enjoy life and know love, you must make yourself available to other people.

Accepting and Recognising

One of the most important pieces of advice to men after separation is that they stop trying to analyse and fix things. Men are used to fixing things, if not with their hands then with their minds. They are born problem solvers and, for them, success often comes from mending what is broken, be it a leaky tap, a failing business or their own relationships. The problem is that sometimes things simply cannot be fixed.

In trying to pick up their life after a break-up, men often fall into two basic categories influenced by our human instinct towards fight or flight. Many men take on their troubles, hitting them with a metaphorical stick in the hopes of beating them. The problem with this 'fight' approach, is that the real target is often their own emotions, which means that they are either taking it out on themselves in the form of self-loathing, self-pity or even self-harm. Men can also misread the whole situation and target someone else with their excess rage – their former wife, children, work, parents or others. The other option is flight. In this mode, men can flee from their troubles – turning to excessive drinking, sleeping around, drugs or other behaviours that can lead to depression, anxiety and, in extreme cases, suicide attempts.

Suicidal Thoughts

One recent study by the National Institute for Healthcare Research indicates that divorced people are three times as likely to commit suicide as people who are married. A study of thirteen European countries by the regional European office of the World Health Organization found that divorce was the only factor linked with suicide in every one of the thirteen countries.

If you think you may hurt yourself or attempt suicide, get help right now by speaking with a friend or loved one or by calling a national suicide helpline number where you will reach a trained counsellor.

If you're feeling suicidal, but you aren't immediately thinking of hurting yourself, seek help by reaching out to a close friend or loved one – even though it may be hard to talk about your feelings. Alternatively, calling any of the national helplines and speaking about your thoughts can be helpful, as is making an appointment with your local doctor. Asking for help can be hard for men, but with treatment this problem can be overcome.

Peter

Peter was a successful forty-seven-year-old civil servant. He had been married for fourteen years with two children, aged thirteen and fourteen, both of whom attended private school.

Peter had been living with his parents since separating from his wife three years before. His mother asked him to seek help, as she was worried about his mental state since his divorce decree six months earlier. On being asked why he was attending counselling, Peter stated that he wanted to try and regain some control over his life. He was tired of feeling bad and wanted to draw a line under his past and move on.

As we talked, Peter kept repeating that he was 'not a bad man'. When I asked him why he thought he was 'bad', he was visibly shocked and replied that he genuinely did not realise he was using that word so much. He stated that for the last twelve years he had listened to his wife complaining to him and about him, particularly about him working too much and his use of bad language in front of the children. He went on to explain that over the years he had become detached from his wife and had fallen out with her family. He conceded that he was verbally abusive, but justified this by saying it only occurred because his wife kept criticising him.

As the sessions continued Peter gradually began to accept that he was not a 'bad' person but that he had faults and that some of his behaviour had not been acceptable. He slowly began to separate out the roles he occupied in life, condensing them down to that of son, husband and father. He acknowledged that he was not a good husband, but also came to recognise that he was a good son, a good father and an overall decent person.

Peter began to understand that his drive to work hard was a primary instinct that had developed in him from an early age: in his mind, if you worked hard you were good and deserved rewards, whereas if you did not work hard you were lazy and deserved to be punished. As we worked together over the months, he was surprised how this thought had come to dominate his thinking and approach to life. Yet here he was, aged forty-seven, sad, lonely and unhappy, even though he had worked hard all his life.

During the sessions, Peter recognised that he was very angry. As we explored his anger, he began to notice that underneath there was also a deep sadness. Like two sides of a coin, he was both angry and sad about how his life had turned out – that he was now back living the role of son after all his hard work to build his own family. At one of our sessions, nearly one year after the divorce, Peter began to cry. He cried for himself, his children and even for his wife. At the end of the session he vowed that he was going to view life and the world from a different angle. He would continue to work hard, but would never again believe that one's value in life was solely related to work. Rather, he would make room for a man called Peter, who tried hard but also made space for love, friends and family.

To consciously live this outlook, he began to take an interest in people and activity outside of work. One simple step was becoming a leader in a local scout troop, of which one of his children was a member. He was successful in this role and began to make links with new people. He went to mediation with his former partner, where they agreed how best to care for their children. By the time therapy ended, Peter was living in his own home and had established a new intimate relationship. He continued to work hard and be successful but ensured that this did not dominate his life.

8

Helping Women Cope

The trauma of relationship breakdown leaves most women experiencing intense emotions. At times they can feel overwhelmed as well as sometimes thinking that they are not coping. The burden of childcare and running the family home usually remains the preserve of the mother. Women are more likely to experience financial hardship than men following the end of a marriage, and research indicates that one year after separation the average woman's income can fall by up to 42 per cent.

This difficult period tests the capacity of most women to care for their psychological and mental health. Usually they put their children's needs before their own. Women I have worked with over the last twenty years reported a range of intense feelings at various stages:

- *Scared* about their responsibility for the economic future of themselves and their children.
- *Sad* about the break-up of their family unit.
- *Nervous* about how they will juggle work and home commitments without the support of a partner.
- *Resentful* about career sacrifices they have made in their role as homemaker.
- *Hateful* towards their former partner.

- *Bitter* about their new circumstances.
- *Worried* about dealing with bureaucracies and the legal system.
- *Fearful* of making the same mistakes in future relationships.
- *Concerned* that the relationship with their former partner may remain in conflict.

These feelings, although distressing, are normal, along with many other emotions and thoughts that could be added to the list. The good news is that most women overcome these feelings and go on to live fulfilling and happy lives. However, this process takes time, patience and endurance.

Research and experience continue to demonstrate that, in general, women are the main purveyors of emotional empathy. Emotional empathy is other-oriented and exhibits the capacity for understanding interpersonal perspectives. In most marriages, it is the emotional intelligence and balance of the woman that indicates the degree of happiness and balance in the relationship.

Generally, separation or divorce occurs following a prolonged period of conflict, where the emotional empathy of the woman towards her partner has slowly worn away. This loss of empathy is a tipping point at which many women come to the conclusion that the relationship is not worth maintaining. Once a woman has decided that she no longer wants to remain in the relationship, she will very often follow through and end it. However, this strength of purpose can often mask a fear for the future and a deep sadness for the lost relationship.

One female client recently described her separation as similar to losing a vital part of her body, a part that had once served her well but no longer worked adequately. After years of struggling and repetitive fighting, she eventually came to the decision that she must let go; that the sooner she completely ended that chapter of her life, the sooner she could set about rebuilding a better life for her children and ultimately finding the happiness most people desire.

Guilt

For many women, guilt can sit quietly behind the anger and worry that come with a broken relationship. An important task for any woman involved in a break-up is to recognise this guilt and to put strategies in place that ensure she does not allow herself to dwell on these negative emotions. It takes two people to make a marriage, and relationships come apart because of the differences of both. No one is perfect, and happiness is a matter of learning from our mistakes. Women who successfully negotiate separation and divorce tend to accept their own shortcomings, set a goal to learn from their experiences and then get on with their life. They come to understand that you will never be comfortable with yourself, nor find real happiness, if you drag feelings of guilt from your past around with you.

To this end, it is important to be clear on the reasons for ending the relationship, so that you are clear of what you want from the future. Between the time that the relationship ends and the time when new happiness is found, women can experience an emotional pain they never dreamed possible. They go through a number of mental and emotional phases, all of which are perfectly normal and necessary in order to heal this great hurt and recover emotional equilibrium. Most female clients report that it is only when they have worked the past out of their system that they begin to heal and open up to the possibility of finding happiness.

It can be helpful to think of everything you are going through in terms of a physical wound: it is going to hurt for some time, but with proper care and attention it will heal. In order that it does so, you must understand the nature of the wound – what to do in order to encourage recovery. It is important to remember that relationship breakdown is not uncommon; that you are not alone, nor going through anything different than a lot of other people have also gone through.

Maintaining Perspective and Setting Goals

It is imperative that a woman detaches herself from the emotional bonds she has established with her former partner as quickly as possible. You can maintain a dignified, dispassionate stance; however, you must stop giving into bouts of negative emotional wrestling. It is just as important to immediately set about analysing what it is you want out of life, and to take the necessary steps towards achieving these goals.

This of course is easier said than done. In the hall of mirrors of a bad relationship, it is easy to lose subjectivity and perspective. In caring for children and their former husband, women can forget what they want for themselves. The first step is to reflect honestly on the relationship, identifying what went wrong and when you stopped achieving your own personal goals and desires. This will ensure you do not enter another relationship without reflecting on your own life goals. In other words, if you do not know what you want, nor how to get it, you will be without purpose and direction in life.

Unless you set goals for yourself, you may not be giving yourself a real chance of happiness. It is vital that you set aside time for reflection: think about yourself and start taking the small steps necessary to becoming proud of the person you are. Even though you are mourning the loss of your marriage, you need to pick yourself up and determine to learn from the experience. From this comes an understanding of where and who you are, and what you have to do in order to move on successfully. Plan it out on paper, and then do what you have to do in order to enact this plan. Do not be afraid of making mistakes once or twice along the way.

Rebuilding your self-esteem and self-confidence is one of the first steps you must take following the end of a relationship. There are many ways to do this; the important thing is that you find something that makes you feel good. It will be difficult, but the sooner a woman starts rejoining a social circle outside of their former spouse, the easier it will be for her to regain emotional well-being. Even though you may have to force yourself at first, you should make a point of associating with other people.

During a relationship breakdown, the most important thing you can do is to move forward sensibly. There are things that can help you on your way back to a fulfilling life:

Think single: You are no longer half of a couple and that can take some getting used to. After all, life as a single woman is very different to the life you have been leading for a major part of your life. Take time to understand the changes that are happening in your life and don't expect it to be easy.

Remind yourself that it is okay to be single: In a society where single and separated women may feel they are being looked down on by their married peers, it is easy for a woman to believe that she is a failure; that 'real' women are involved in loving, lasting relationships. That is simply not true. More and more women are choosing to remain single, or to break out of unfulfilling relationships. This demonstrates strength rather than weakness. You must believe in yourself as a person in your own right.

Don't try to get even: No matter how angry you are at your former partner – even if he has been unfaithful to you – do not try to get your own back. You will only end up exhausting your personal energy on something that will not be the least bit fruitful. The bitterness will most likely stop you from moving on, and you don't deserve that. Try to approach your anger in a sensible manner, one that helps you get back to a healthy state of mind. Writing down exactly what is making you angry and why can often help in dealing with these feelings. Find a friend who will listen, or consult a therapist, and tell them how you feel. Anger needs an outlet, but revenge is not a healthy way of venting it.

Accept that the relationship is over: When you are living alone and your former partner has 'moved on', it should be easy to accept that it is over. Unfortunately, this is something that a lot of women have difficulty with. You may find yourself making excuses to visit your former partner – forgetting things at his place or needing to discuss something trivial regarding your son/daughter. By all means, talk to him when you need to and visit if you must, but keep your distance emotionally and accept that you now lead separate lives.

Don't live in the past: No doubt you have some great memories from your time together – you would never have stayed together as long as you did if there weren't good times – but do not dwell on them. If you find yourself wishing that everything could be 'like the old days', remind yourself that there are fantastic moments waiting for you in the future. You can learn from the past, but you cannot change it or return to it. The future is what you should be thinking about now.

Don't give in to guilt: In the course of the break-up you probably said a few things you did not mean and now regret, but that cannot be changed. By all means apologise to your former partner – it may make you feel better – but the most important thing is that you forgive yourself and learn from your mistakes.

Rediscover yourself: How much of yourself did you give up during your relationship? Did you find yourself bending over backwards to satisfy your partner? Now is the time to start living for you! By doing the things that make you happy, you will increase your self-confidence. Do anything you like, but do it for you.

Sort out your finances: Your financial situation is bound to have changed and it is important that you know exactly how much you have coming in. It can be easy to start over-spending when you are in a period of self-pity, with extra indulgences here and there. But getting into debt will only make your life even more difficult. If your income is low (or non-existent), contact the appropriate government agencies and find out about assistance. They will have somebody available to assess your needs and help you claim any benefits that you may be eligible for.

Don't get involved in rebound relationships: Most people know this is a bad idea, but when you meet a new man soon after a break-up, it can be easy to forget. After years of perhaps not feeling loved, and now during this period of sadness, your judgement is not at its best. With this in mind, keep your dates light and remember that there is a big difference between getting to know a new person and forming a close, intimate relationship. When you try to skip from one to the other too quickly you force the relationship, and forced relationships rarely last. It is true that some whirlwind romances survive the test of time, but those are the exception rather than the rule.

A New Way of Seeing

Following a break-up, women can be confronted with many challenges: financial troubles, loneliness, grief. Coping with and recovering from relationship breakdown requires a new way of seeing just about everything in your life. Key to this is forgiveness and the ability to move on.

All healing begins with forgiveness. However, when the actions of your former partner are the reason your life is so irrevocably changed, it may seem reasonable to think that that person doesn't deserve forgiveness. The main point of forgiveness, though, is to set yourself free, not to let the guilty party off the hook. By forgiving, you are not condoning their behaviour, you are saying, 'I choose not to live with the feelings of bitterness.' When you hold on to hurt feelings, you are hurting yourself far more than you are hurting the person who hurt you. In fact, by letting go of any anger you feel towards them, you destroy your former partner's power to keep hurting you.

Latitude and Gratitude

A second approach that will help you move forward is that of latitude and gratitude. This simple but powerful concept is key in finding and maintaining emotional well-being. Ask yourself what you are thankful for. It may seem hard to find hope after a broken relationship, but even in the darkest of times there is probably something for which you can feel grateful. It could be something as simple as the kind words of a friend or the smile of a child. No matter how hard the relationship was or how devastating its end, the fact that your son or daughter exists as a result is a reason to feel gratitude.

Seek Help

Finally, do not be ashamed to seek help. The fact that you are reading this book indicates that you know there is help available, and this should encourage you. There are many sources for help, including support groups and counselling. Sharing your thoughts with others is invaluable and just knowing you are not alone can make a world of difference. Give yourself time to grieve the loss of the future you had imagined. Then, with a little help from your friends, move on with a new outlook. The results are up to you.

> **Jane**
>
> Jane was faced with a divorce after thirty-three years of marriage. At our first session she described it as an event that took her vision of what she thought her life would be and turned it into 'an embarrassing, tragic soap opera'. When I asked her to describe in one word how she felt, she said 'overwhelmed'. She described how she could not see her life ever being good again, or how she would recover – or even just get a good night's sleep. She felt betrayed and rejected and could not make sense of her life following the separation and subsequent divorce.

Initially, Jane moved between anger and sadness as she expressed her thoughts about her husband, who she believed took the best years of her life and then left her when she was no longer the pretty twenty-one-year-old he had married. In early sessions, she conveyed confusion and a complete disbelief at her situation. She spent agonising days and sleepless nights of trying to come to terms with the fact her marriage was over.

She spoke of her rage and bitterness, and spent long periods ruminating on how she could give her former husband a glimpse of the pain he had caused for so many people. Jane didn't know how to stop the downward spiral, or if she could get back to even a moderately decent life again. She kept replaying scenes and conversations in her head, trying to figure out what went wrong, what she should have done differently and what she was supposed to do now.

In a strange way, it was her determination not to let her former husband see her as a broken, sad person that motivated Jane to overcome her grief and gain control of her life again. In one session she said, 'I don't want him to see how broken I am by the whole thing.' As we worked through her thoughts and feelings, Jane began to articulate how she was learning lessons about life because of the divorce, not in spite of it. She had moved from focusing on her loss to thinking about actions and people that could restore her faith in life.

Jane had learned that no matter how much she obsessed over past events, they would not change. She made a conscious decision not to let the past dominate her life; rather she decided that her energy was much better spent in the present moment. She chose to move forward towards something good, rather than continue on in the role of victim. She detached from her husband psychologically. She captured this change succinctly when she said: 'What he did in the past does not matter. What matters is what I am doing right now.'

She worked on some simple mindfulness techniques, and took some time every morning and evening to practise them. She did not judge her life as good or bad, just accepted it and concentrated on being thankful in that moment. She gradually got into a habit of living in the moment and moved away from allowing herself to be led by knee-jerk reactions. Rather than getting up every morning and crying or becoming angry, Jane set about the task of taking care of herself.

She actively sought out the support of other women and began sharing experiences, questions and solutions. She found that other women were facing and overcoming the same issues she was. By the end of therapy, Jane had learned life-changing lessons and tried to live every day with serenity and a level of freedom she never thought she would experience again.

Coping and Recovering Through Mindfulness

Relationship breakdown is stressful, and clients often describe feeling adrift, continuously swimming against a psychological current or being bashed about in an emotional whirlpool. About ten years ago I was introduced to mindfulness. The simplicity of the practice caught my attention. I researched and developed techniques that clients could learn and use in their daily life in between therapy sessions. It became evident that when given the right amount of information and knowledge, clients very quickly learned and developed a capacity to observe themselves and watch their stream of consciousness, rather than being buffeted by its currents. The key message from clients was to keep it simple, as once they grasped the basics they tended to feel better. However, if information and exercises were too detailed and over-complicated, people tended not to use this approach.

Trying to understand mindfulness by its definition is like trying to understand what it is like to fall in love by reading a book. You might get a general idea, but you'd be missing out on the best part: what it actually *feels* like. Mindfulness is all about the actual aliveness of each moment, learning to pay attention to your unfolding experience. It is both a spiritual and psychological state of being in which we attend to our thoughts and emotions. The establishing of mindfulness in day-to-day life helps to maintain a calm awareness of one's body, feelings and mind.

Mindfulness means paying non-judgemental attention in the present moment. When we practise mindfulness we can get in touch with life more deeply; we have much less tendency to get caught up in thinking about the past and thinking about what might happen in the future. Mindfulness allows us to take control of our lives so that we are not slaves to our previously conditioned responses. We have all experienced moments of great clarity in our lives, by looking at a sunrise, a personal photograph, a beautiful flower or our child's face. These are moments of mindfulness. At a time of great change, the cultivation of mindfulness facilitates awareness of these beautiful moments on a regular basis and can profoundly enrich our lives with a greater sense of well-being and happiness.

Coming Off Automatic Pilot

Even though we have always been right here, in this life, we often don't truly notice life. Rather we get caught in the humdrum of daily existence. We can live on a kind of automatic pilot mode, where we travel through our days without really paying attention to anything. We travel to and from work, and at the end of our commute it is almost as if it didn't happen. It is sort of like sleepwalking. Yet nobody would suspect that we are barely there – maybe because they're on automatic pilot too. Spend enough time on automatic pilot and life begins to feel shallow. Add to this the psychological turmoil of a relationship breakdown and people begin to learn that something is missing and something has to change.

Could it be that the missing ingredient is ourselves? When we are not paying attention to the present moment we are absent from our own life. Practical mindfulness, and the meditation-based practices that are used to cultivate it, are a way to reconnect with what is most vital and alive in our experience. It is a way to fully experience ourselves and our world.

At the simplest level, it is putting aside three minutes each day to do nothing but pay attention to how you are; to stop, breathe and feel. Let the past be over and done with and let what has not yet happened be off in the future. This practice is about recognising and accepting where you are right now. Just give yourself three minutes to feel your body and mind. Of course, you might not find what you expect, or what you want. Give yourself a chance to be surprised. You might notice that your mind wanders constantly and that you have one restless thought after another. You might notice that there is a longing in your heart, or a dream that is asking to be fulfilled. Right now, you don't need to do anything about whatever it is that you find. The goal isn't to have any particular experience, but rather to check in with how it really is to be you. The practice of mindfulness begins with learning to check your own inner compass. Slow down, just for a few minutes. When you know where you are right now, your next steps become a lot clearer.

Some Basic Concepts
Breath
Mindfulness of breathing uses the breath as an object of concentration. By focusing on the breath you become aware of the mind's tendency to jump from one thing to another. The simple discipline of concentration on the

breath brings us back to the present moment and all the richness of experience that it contains. It is a way to develop mindfulness, the faculty of alert and sensitive awareness and a good antidote to restlessness and anxiety. It is a good way to relax and has a positive effect on your entire physical and mental state.

Body
Mindfulness of the body tunes into the sensations in the body in the present moment. In practising mindfulness of the body, it is your direct experience or felt sense that is important; not your judgements about your body, your wishes for what it might be, or even your stories about how your body came to be as it is. The body is the storehouse of all the physical and emotional events of your life to this point, starting with your genetic inheritance. Through reflection you gain the insight that these conditions, while unique to you, are actually impersonal, like conditions in nature, and that clinging to them with anger, resentfulness or self-pity only adds to your suffering. Your liberation lies not in what the body has stored from the past but in how you respond to whatever manifests in your body in any given moment.

Thoughts
See thoughts as 'just thinking', without feeding or fighting them. When we practise mindfulness of the body or the breath, we are already doing something different. We are bringing awareness into a situation. That simple act weakens the power of our automatic pilot as we accept and recognise our thoughts without reacting to them. The practice of mindfulness defuses our negativity, aggression and turbulent emotions because rather than suppressing

emotions or indulging in them, we just recognise and accept them.

Emotions
We spend our life reacting to thoughts and emotions or taking substances to play them up or dampen them down. The internal struggle to put something out of your mind usually results in increased tension and a rebound phenomenon where the avoided thought or feeling returns even stronger. Mindfulness allows us to stay present to the unpleasant thought or feeling for its natural duration without feeding or repressing it.

When we accept and recognise emotions, including anxiety, shame, anger, sadness or distress, we replace fear and avoidance with curiosity about their exact nature – their quality and how they change as time passes. In this way we learn that negative thoughts and feelings are transitory. Trust me, a few moments of mindfulness is a better mood enhancer than a glass of your favourite wine or beer.

Solutions
As the grip of automatic pilot on the mind is relaxed we become more free to act with and tap into other parts of our brain. Our unconscious mind can then process information differently and present us with spontaneously arising wisdom, as we are more able to access creative responses when we are less absorbed in our mental chatter. Think of a football player who carries out a skilful move that he has never done before in a high-pressure game; think of the great works of art, unplanned but brilliant; or indeed the beauty of ocean that inspires calm and serenity.

Avoid Mirroring

Emotions of all sorts are contagious when we live on autopilot. This can be very enjoyable when we are sharing positive emotions. However, it can also mean we feed off each other's shame, anger, fear or depression. There is a neurological process that supports this mutual imitation – mammals, including humans, have a system of 'mirror neurons' which fire both when we perform a particular action and when we perceive someone else perform that same action.

Mindfulness allows us to stay present to other people without being caught up in or mirroring destructive emotions. Rather we learn to respond in a wiser, simpler and subtler way. With practice, we can learn to stay present to any situation instead of acting on autopilot. This very humble approach can interrupt escalation of destructive emotions by dampening emotional contagion and create a very positive outcome for all affected by relationship breakdown.

Appreciate Life

Mindfulness tends to make life activities more fulfilling. Intrinsically pleasant experiences (food, music, sex, etc.) become more intense and satisfying simply because one is more fully 'in the moment'. Furthermore, ordinary experiences (washing dishes, driving to work, etc.) take on a quality of vibrancy as fear and boredom become a thing of the past.

It is incredible what an impact learning to truly notice your sense and environment can have on your life. By becoming mindful of who, what and where we are, we can experience increased balance and contentment at a time when life is not what you had hoped or planned for. During separation and divorce the mind gets pulled from one place to the next, leaving you feeling stressed, confused and disorganised. However, it is very important for your health to allow yourself a few minutes here and there for mental spaciousness.

Exercises

Mindfulness can be practised both formally and informally. Informally, by spending time recognising and appreciating the everyday activities that we take for granted; and formally within meditation and other contemplative disciplines. Below are a number of exercises to help empty your mind for a few minutes and find some relief and clarity amidst the turmoil of relationship breakdown.

Exercise 1: Imagery

Sit in a comfortable position and close your eyes. Focus on your breathing, paying attention to the way your belly rises with each breath in and falls with each breath out. Feel as if you're floating on the waves of your own breathing. If your mind wanders elsewhere, gently return to it. Now listen to the sounds around you – maybe the music playing on the stereo, a noise next door or sounds outside. Don't strain to listen. Just hear the sounds that come your way and accept them, without thinking about what they mean. Listen to the silences between sounds too.

Exercise 2: One-Minute Breathing

This exercise can be done anywhere at any time. It is particularly useful if you are due to meet your former partner or attend a potentially stressful event. All you have to do is focus on your breathing for just one minute. Breathe in and out slowly, holding your breath for a count of six as you inhale. Naturally, your mind will try and wander, but just try to focus on the rise and fall of your breath and let thoughts go as they arise. Watch the breath as it enters your body and fills you with life, and then watch it leave effortlessly from your body as the energy dissipates into the universe.

Exercise 3: Mindful Observation

This exercise is simple but incredibly powerful. Clients find it especially useful to carry out when alone at the end of the day. Pick out a feature within your immediate natural environment and focus on watching it for one minute (this could be a flower, a cloud or the moon). Let thoughts of anything else in your life drop away as you concentrate and visually explore this glorious feature of the natural world.

Exercise 4: The Apple

Have an apple (or another piece of fresh fruit that you like) on hand. Sit in a comfortable position. Take a few deep breaths, and relax your body. Focus on what is happening in the here and now, and let go of other thoughts. Now focus your attention on the apple. Notice its colour, shape, texture and smell. Take a bite, and notice the flavour as if you had never tasted an apple before. Return your thoughts to the apple whenever your mind starts to wander. Enjoy the feelings of pleasure that arise as you experience eating mindfully.

Exercise 5: Touch Points

During relationship breakdown we have a tendency to dwell on what we have lost. This exercise helps move the mind to think of something that happens every day more than once; something you take for granted, like opening the front door as you leave for work, for example. At that moment when you touch the doorknob, allow yourself to be completely mindful of where you are, how you feel and what you are doing. The cues don't have to be physical; it could be that every time you think something negative, you take a mindful moment to release the negative thought. Or it could be that every time you smell food you take a mindful moment to rest in the appreciation of having food to eat. Choose a touch point that resonates with you today, and stop and stay with it for a while.

Exercise 6: Mindful Listening

This exercise is useful at the start or end of the day. Choose a new piece of music, something you've never heard before. Don't think about the genre or the artist, instead just allow yourself to get lost in the journey of sound for the duration of the song. The idea is to just listen, to do nothing else but hear, without preconception or judgement. If you can't find any music you like, simply listen to the sounds in your environment. Don't try and determine what the sounds are, just listen and absorb the experience.

Exercise 7: Fully Experience a Regular Routine

Take a regular routine that you don't think much about and make it a mindful one. For example, when cleaning your house or car, pay attention to every detail of cleaning. Be mindful of what you are doing. Watch and feel the motion of sweeping the floor or scrubbing the dishes. Be in the moment, aware and present. Don't simply clean on autopilot as you usually would; feel your way through the routine and merge with the activity, physically and mentally.

Exercise 8: Take Five

In this mindfulness exercise, all you need to do is notice five things in your day that usually go unnoticed. These could be things you hear, smell, feel or see. For example, you might see the walls, hear the birds, feel your clothes or smell the flowers. Of course, you may already do these things, but are you really aware of these things and the connections they have with your world?

Being in Your Body

People who endure relationship breakdown come to realise that there is no ideal or perfection. A lot of clients learn that they need to accept themselves for who they are and how they appear. In the modern world it is amazing how we can be completely preoccupied with the appearance of our own body and at the same time completely out of touch with it. Relationship breakdown can reawaken some of our deep-seated insecurity about how we look. Clients often speak of how they grew up feeling awkward and unattractive, disliking their body for one reason or another. Usually it was because there was an 'ideal' look they felt someone else had that they didn't. Sooner or later, most people get over such particular adolescent preoccupations, but the root insecurity can remain. Many adults feel that their body is either too fat or too short or too tall or too old or too 'ugly', as if there was some perfect way that it should be. Sadly we may never feel completely comfortable with the way our body is. We may never feel completely at home in it. And as we get older, this malaise may be compounded by the awareness that our body is ageing. Following a relationship breakdown these fears are often magnified. Yet the reality is that your approach to your body can't change until you actually experience your body. When we put energy into actually experiencing our body and refuse to get caught up in judgmental thinking about it, our whole view of it and of ourself can change dramatically. So, before you continue with the autopilot thoughts that you body is 'too this' or 'too that', you need to get more in touch with how wonderful it is to have a body in the first place, no matter what it looks or feels like.

The way to do this is to tune in to your body and be mindful of it without judging it. You have already begun this process by becoming mindful of your breathing, your thoughts and your surroundings; now it is time to pay attention to the sensations your body generates. These sensations are usually tuned out because they are so familiar. When you tune in to them, you are reclaiming your own life in that moment, and your own body – making yourself more real and more alive.

Exercise 9: Minding Your Body

This exercise is a very powerful technique to re-establish contact with your body. It is an effective technique for developing concentration and flexibility of attention simultaneously. It involves lying on your back and moving your mind through the different regions of your body. We start with the toes of the left foot and slowly move up the foot and leg, feeling the sensations as we go and directing the breath into and out of the different regions. From the pelvis, we go to the toes of the right foot and move up the right leg back to the pelvis. From there, we move up through the torso, through the lower back and abdomen, the upper back and chest, and the shoulders. Then we go to the fingers of both hands and move up simultaneously in both arms, returning to the shoulders.

Then we move through the neck and throat, and finally all the regions of the face, the back of the head, and the top of the head. We wind up breathing through an imaginary 'hole' in the very top of the head.

The idea is to actually feel each region you focus on and linger there with your mind right on it or in it. You breathe into and out from each region a few times and then let go of it in your mind's eye as your attention moves on to the next region. As you let go of the sensations you find in each region and of any of the thoughts and/or images you may have found associated with it, the muscles in that region literally let go too, lengthening and releasing much of the tension they have accumulated. It helps if you can feel or imagine that the tension in your body and the feelings of fatigue associated with it are flowing out on each out-breath and that on each in-breath you are breathing in energy, vitality and relaxation.

We let our breathing move through the entire body from one end to the other, as if it were flowing in through the top of the head and out through the toes, and then in through the toes and out through the top of the head. It can feel as if the entire body has dropped away or has become transparent, as if its substance were in some way erased. It can feel as if there is nothing but breath flowing freely across all the boundaries of the body. As you complete the exercise, just dwell in silence and stillness, in an awareness that may have by this point gone beyond the body altogether. After a time, when you feel ready to, you return to your body, to a sense of it as a whole. You feel it as solid again. You move your hands and feet and might also massage the face and rock a little from side to side before opening your eyes and returning to the activities of the day. Practise the body scan at least once a day, six days per week.

Clients find this exercise a very useful approach for a number of reasons. First, it is done lying down. That makes it more comfortable and therefore more doable than sitting up straight for forty-five minutes. Many people find it easier, especially at the beginning, to go into a deep state of relaxation when they are lying down. In addition, the inner work of healing is greatly enhanced if you can develop your ability to place your attention systematically anywhere in your body that you want it to go and to direct energy there. This requires a degree of sensitivity to your body and to the sensations you experience from its various regions. In conjunction with your breathing, the exercise is a perfect vehicle for developing and refining this kind of sensitivity. For many people it provides the first positive experience of their body that they have had for many years.

At the same time, mindfulness of the body cultivates moment-to-moment awareness. Each time the mind wanders, we bring it back to the part of the body that we were working with when it drifted off, just as we bring the mind back to the breath when it wanders in the sitting meditation. When you practise mindfulness regularly, you come to notice that your body isn't quite the same every time you do it. You become aware that your body is changing constantly, that even the sensations in, say, your toes, may be different each time you practise or even from one moment to the next.

Through repeated practice of mindfulness techniques and exercises, one can come to grasp the reality of our body as whole in the present moment. The key point is to maintain awareness in every moment, a detached witnessing of your breath and your body, region by region, as you scan from your feet to the top of your head. The quality of your attention and your willingness just to feel what is there and be with it no matter what is the most important factor in mindfulness. If you are practising being present in each moment and, at the same time, you are allowing your breathing and your attention to purify the body within this context of awareness and with a willingness to accept whatever happens, then you are truly practising mindfulness and tapping its power to help you heal and recover.

The distinction is important. The best way to benefit from mindfulness is not to try to get anything from it but just to do it for its own sake. We practise in this way because the effort to try to 'get somewhere' is so often the wrong kind of effort for catalysing change or growth or healing, coming as it usually does from a rejection of present-moment reality without having a full awareness and understanding of that reality.

A desire for things to be other than the way they actually are is simply wishful thinking. It is not a very effective way of bringing about real change. At the first signs of what you think is 'failure' – when you feel that you are not getting anywhere or have not gotten to where you think you should be – you are likely to become discouraged or feel overwhelmed, lose hope, blame external forces and give up. Therefore no real change ever happens.

The mindful view is that it is only through the acceptance of the actuality of the present – no matter how painful, frightening or undesirable it may be – that change, growth and healing can come about. New possibilities exist within your present-moment reality, they only need to be nurtured in order to unfold and be discovered.

Conclusion

Unfortunately, relationship breakdown is a common part of modern family life for many and is an undeniably difficult experience. However, we now know that with the right approach, knowledge and information, one can not only overcome the challenges of relationship breakdown but indeed discover a new inner strength and insight from the experience.

Over the years, I have helped a lot of good people overcome their struggles with relationship breakdown. Given the right support, I have observed these clients learn and create a better future both for themselves and for their children, some examples of which I have shared with you in this book.

As you finish reading, keep in mind all the points raised in the previous chapters. Ahead of you lies a new road that is not in keeping with how you planned your life. However, by adhering to the principles and practices you have read, be assured that a new life of hope and possibility is available to you and your family.

In the first instance, remember that when a relationship ends it can be very hard to move beyond the conflict. Yet we now know that conflict will not enable recovery; rather it will continue to hurt you and stop you putting your energy into creating a better, more fulfilling life for you and your children. Be clear in your mind that overcoming relationship breakdown will reawaken aspects of your life that may have vanished during your failing relationship. Be assured it is possible to replace the sorrow of a failed relationship with confidence and hope for the future.

As you move forward with your life, try not to become caught up in the cultural script that says everybody will meet their true love and live happily ever after. In reality, maintaining a lifelong intimate relationship is a challenge that, as you now know, can end in disappointment, despite best intentions.

Finally, it is important that you actively embrace and attend to your emotional and psychological health. This can be done on your own or with the help of a counsellor. Individuals who have good emotional health are aware of their thoughts, feelings and behaviours. They cope with stress and problems in healthy ways. Achieving emotional health will help you improve and strengthen your resilience for the journey ahead, help you cope with stress better and give you a more positive perspective of yourself.

Relationship breakdown is a testing journey on which you need to recognise, appreciate and care for yourself. At times you will be overwhelmed, struggling and questioning your capacity for love and contentment. Be prepared to accept the emotions that you encounter along the way. Do not ignore your thoughts and feelings but accept and recognise them. Relationship breakdown, although difficult, creates choices in how you will live your life from here on out. It forces you out of the shallow waters of daily existence to reflect on deeper issues. Be prepared to engage in spiritual and mindful acts rather than pushing things away. Trust me, engaging in what you are going through with mindfulness will give you a better perspective and approach to help you cope and recover.

Finally, the secret to getting the most out of this book is to read, reflect and work to change your behaviour and thinking. Personal growth is the key to ensuring a successful outcome to relationship breakdown, after which you can set out on a new path to contentment. Remember that when pain, anger or hopelessness descend, you can and will recover.

Further Reading and Resources

Books and Articles

Ahrons, Constance R., *We're Still Family: What Grown Children Have To Say About Their Parents' Divorce* (New York: HarperCollins, 2004).

Biddulph, Steve, *Manhood* (London: Vermillion, 2004).

Blaisure, K. R. and M. J. Geasler, 'Results of a Survey of Court-Connected Parent Education Programs in U.S. Counties, *Family and Conciliation Courts Review* (1996).

Bryan, Mark, *The Prodigal Father: Reuniting Fathers and Their Children* (Sydney: Three Rivers Press, 1997).

Farrelly, John, *The Art of Balance: Creating Calm in a Chaotic World* (Dublin: Veritas, 2008).

—, *The Good Marriage Guide: The Practical Way to Improve Your Relationship* (Dublin, Veritas, 2007).

Garber, Benjamin, *Keeping Kids Out of the Middle: Child-Centred Parenting in the Midst of Conflict, Separation and Divorce* (Deerfield Beach, FL: Health Communications Inc., 2008).

Golden, Thomas R., *Swallowed by a Snake: The Gift of the Masculine Side of Healing* (London: Golden Healing Publishing, 1996).

Hetherington, E. Mavis, 'Intimate Pathways: Changing Patterns in Close Personal Relationships Across Time', *Family Relations* 52 (2003): 318–31.

Kposowa, Augustine, 'Marital Status and Suicide in the National Longitudinal Mortality Study', *Journal of Epidemiology and Community Health*, 54.4 (2000): 254–61.

McKeown, K., T. Haase and J. Pratschke, *Unhappy Marriages: Does Counselling Help?* (Dublin: ACCORD, 2004).

Smith, Peter K., *The Psychology of Grandparenthood: An International Perspective*, (London: Routledge, 1991).

Timonen, V., M. Doyle and D. O'Dwyer, *Grandparents in Divorced and Separated Families* (Dublin: Trinity College, 2009).

Tomlin, Angela M., 'Grandparents' Influences on Grandchildren', *Handbook on Grandparenthood*, M. E. Szinovacz, ed. (Westport, CT: Greenwood Publishing,1998).

Townsend, Peter, *The Family Life of Old People* (London: Routledge, 1957).

Uhlenberg, P. and B. G. Hammill, 'Frequency of Grandparent Contact with Grandchild Sets: Six Factors That Make a Difference', *Gerontologist* 38.3 (1998): 276–85.

Wallerstein, Judith S. and Joan Berlin Kelly, *Surviving the Breakup: How Children and Parents Cope With Divorce* (New York: Basic Books, 1980).

Websites

Achieve Balance Counselling Service
http://www.achievebalance.ie

Child Centered Divorce
http://www.childcentereddivorce.com

Collaborative Law
http://www.collaborativelaw.com

Co-Parenting
http://www.2houses.com

Grandparents
http://www.grandparents.com

Mediation
http://www.familymediation.ie

Relationships
http://www.accord.ie
http://www.relate.org.uk

Parenting
http://www.handinhandparenting.org
http://www.parenting.com